# JONATHAN
# EDWARDS

# JONATHAN EDWARDS

## A Guided Tour
## of His Life and Thought

STEPHEN J. NICHOLS

Foreword by
Samuel T. Logan Jr.

P U B L I S H I N G
P.O. BOX 817 • PHILLIPSBURG • NEW JERSEY 08865-0817

*Page design and typesetting by Lakeside Design Plus*

Printed in the United States of America

**Library of Congress Cataloging-in-Publication Data**

Nichols, Stephen J., 1970-
    Jonathan Edwards : a guided tour of his life & thought / Stephen J. Nichols.
        p.    cm.
    Includes bibliographical references and index.
    ISBN 0-87552-194-0 (pbk.)
    1. Edwards, Jonathan, 1703–1758. I. Title.
BX7260.E3 N53 2001
285.8'092—dc21
    [B]                                                       2001036323

For Heidi

*The young lady in Lancaster,*
*beloved of the Almighty Being.*

# CONTENTS

# FOREWORD

The Doctor, D. Martyn Lloyd-Jones, made this claim with regard to the importance of Jonathan Edwards: "I am tempted, perhaps foolishly, to compare the Puritans to the Alps, Luther and Calvin to the Himalayas, and Jonathan Edwards to Mount Everest! He has always seemed to me the man most like the Apostle Paul."

Extravagant? Perhaps. But then again, perhaps not.

Lloyd-Jones saw correctly that there was something very, very special about Edwards and about his contributions to our understanding of some of the fundamental truths of the Christian faith and, even more specifically, of some of the unique discoveries and emphases of the Reformed faith.

Lloyd-Jones continued his appraisal of Edwards with this advice: "So read this man. Decide to do so. Read his sermons; read his practical treatises, and then go on to the great discourses on theological subjects." This is surely some of the best advice anyone could give or receive.

But easier said than done!

Eighteenth-century ecclesiastical culture differed from what we know in the new, twenty-first century. The specific issues were different, and the language used to discuss them was different. It simply is the case that reading Edwards today requires special effort and special assistance.

In *Jonathan Edwards: A Guided Tour of His Life and Thought,* Stephen Nichols provides exactly the kind of assistance that is needed—a clear summary of Edwards's major themes set against the background of his life and the struggles faced by the church to which he was called to minister. In this easily read and relatively brief guide, Nichols does an excellent job of preparing the reader to gain the most from reading Edwards himself.

At Westminster Theological Seminary (and many other seminaries, I am sure), students often become impatient with the required extensive training in Hebrew and Greek that precedes their training in exegesis. They want to get at the text of Scripture right away, and that is a good desire. But their work with the text of Scripture is invariably richer and deeper and more beneficial to them and the churches they ultimately serve if they first learn the languages in which Scripture was written.

So it is with Edwards. Lloyd-Jones was right: it is ultimately Edwards we all should read. But Nichols's book will make any reading of Edwards invariably richer and deeper and more beneficial to both the individual reader and those to whom the reader ministers.

But lest means to an end be confused with the end itself, we must remind ourselves that we do not read even Edwards for Edwards's sake. We read Edwards because Edwards interprets Scripture so powerfully that he helps us to see God better. The end for Edwards—and for Nichols and for us—is always the same. I return to Lloyd-Jones one more time. After urging us to read Edwards, the Doctor explains why:

> But above all, let all of us, preachers and listeners, having read this man, let us try to capture and to lay hold upon his greatest emphasis of all—the glory of God. Let us not stop at

any benefit we may have had, and not even with the highest experiences we may have enjoyed. Let us seek to know more and more of the glory of God. We need to know the majesty of God, the sovereignty of God, and to feel a sense of awe and wonder. Do we know this? Is there in our churches a sense of wonder and of amazement? This is the impression Jonathan Edwards always conveys and creates.

Reading Nichols will prepare us better to read Edwards, who gives us magnificent visions of the glory and beauty of our majestic, sovereign God.

It is thus with enthusiasm that I commend both this book and the writings of Edwards himself.

Samuel T. Logan Jr.
Westminster Theological Seminary (PA)

Note: The quotations from D. Martyn Lloyd-Jones are from his paper "Jonathan Edwards and the Critical Importance of Revival," in *The Puritan Experiment in the New World*, pages 103–21. His paper and others in this volume were delivered at the 1976 Westminster Conference, London, England.

# ILLUSTRATIONS

# PREFACE

This book began as an idea expressed over a dinner conversation with Bryce Craig, president of P&R, three years ago. Since (and even before) then, many people have helped that idea develop into this book. It is my singular joy to offer them my heartfelt thanks.

I am especially grateful to my many teachers. George S. Claghorn of West Chester University casually suggested that I write my master's thesis on Jonathan Edwards, starting me on a journey I have thoroughly enjoyed. The faculty at Westminster Theological Seminary blended godliness and scholarship in a way that would make Edwards feel right at home. Samuel T. Logan Jr. not only graciously taught me about Edwards, but also supplied the foreword for this book. For both, I am grateful.

I am also grateful to various friends and colleagues. Sean Lucas is both a good friend and a great sounding board. Douglas A. Sweeney, Glenn Kreider, Donald Westblade, and others in the Jonathan Edwards Study Group are truly congenial scholars and friends. My pastor, Michael Rogers, also deserves a grateful thanks for his constant encouragement. On Sundays I feel as though I have left Lancaster for Northampton. At Lancaster Bible College, Ray Naugle has enthusiastically supported this project, which I appreciate. I am also grateful to Jim McGahey for his stimulating conversations and encouragement. Finally, Al Fisher at P&R has made the writing and publishing of this book a pleasure.

I am also grateful to my parents, George and K. Diane Nichols, for providing a godly and loving home. They introduced me to the delightful and rewarding habit of buying and reading books, and they have been a constant encouragement throughout my studies, teaching, and writing. I also wish to thank my in-laws, Keith and Beverly Haselhorst, for their friendship, encouragement, and love.

Finally, I want to express my gratitude to and love for my wife, Heidi. She has patiently and graciously supported me through a thesis, a dissertation, and now a book on Edwards. Her thorough proofreading and encouragement have made this a truly collaborative effort. It is fitting that we have made a place for Edwards in our home, as he and my wife share the same birthday. She also shares his passion for Christ. I am grateful for her example, love, and friendship, and it is to her that I dedicate this book.

# INTRODUCTION

## *The Perennial Edwards*

*There is urgent need of a new generation who will
take up and read Edwards.*
                              —Iain H. Murray

*The remarkable feature of Edwards . . . is his enduring
ability to speak across the ages.*
                              —Harry S. Stout

I remember the first time I tried to read Jonathan Edwards. I was visiting a college and sat in on a church history class. That day there happened to be a guest lecturer on Edwards. He ended his lecture by issuing a challenge to read *Religious Affections,* claiming that, next to Scripture, it stands as the single most important book for any Christian to grapple with. I was persuaded. I bought the book and started to read it. I did not finish it, and I'm not sure what I got out of it. The problem, however, was not with Edwards. To be sure, his writing can be difficult for a contemporary audience, but it is not impossible. Nor was the problem that Edwards had nothing meaningful to say. In his powdered wig and Geneva bands he may look as if he has nothing to say to us, but I believed then—and I still do now—that he has much to say to us today.

The problem was with me. I knew of Edwards. I knew that he was a colonial New England minister, that he was a key figure in the Great Awakening, and that he briefly served as president of Princeton before his life was tragically cut short. But that is about all I knew. I did not know what ideas had captivated his attention throughout his life or what struggles he was involved in. I did not know the details of the events that shaped his thought, or the way he served to shape events and the thought of others. And I certainly did not know what he was trying to do in *Religious Affections.*

That is precisely why I am writing this book. This book is built on the conviction, which I first learned from that guest lecturer, that Edwards must be read because he has many valuable things to say to us. It is also built on the conviction that Edwards can be read, especially with a little help. I suspect that most people in evangelical churches know something of Edwards. I further suspect that many would like to know more, but they are uncertain where to begin. So I offer this book as an introduction, a gateway into the vast and rewarding life, thought, and writings of Jonathan Edwards. It is not an end in itself; it is not a substitute for reading Edwards. It is intended to help anyone who, like me, has wanted to read Edwards and even has tried to read him, but needs a little help.

This, of course, begs the question of both the relevance and importance of Jonathan Edwards. Recently one scholar spoke of the perennial Edwards, pointing to his continuing impact on American theology and thought. Given the wealth of material on and about Edwards, I think he is right. In fact, since the 1950s or so, approximately three thousand books, dissertations, and articles have been written on Edwards. Why do so many people find him interesting? Let me offer five reasons.

First, his personal life is intriguing. He was the only brother to ten sisters. His father, father-in-law, grandfather, one of his sons, one of his sons-in-law, and several grandsons, uncles, and nephews were all ministers. He was also the grandfather of America's third vice president—who also holds his place in history for inflicting a mortal wound on Alexander Hamilton in a duel. Edwards distinguished himself as a young scholar, secured one of New England's most prestigious pulpits at the age of twenty-six, and then, ironically, was voted out after twenty-two years of ministry. He served as a missionary to Native Americans and concluded his life as president of Princeton.

The loving relationship he enjoyed with his wife is legendary. When he first met her, he was enraptured by her and sketched some rather poetic lines extolling her virtues in the flyleaf of a book. At the time of his death, he referred to, as often quoted, "the uncommon union" he was blessed to have with Sarah. And he was a loving father, as evidenced in the gracious and warm correspondence he carried on with his eleven children. During the height of the Great Awakening, many demands were placed on Edwards in addition to his already full schedule. Yet he always devoted portions of the day to giving undivided attention to his children.

In addition, he mentored half of New England as young candidates for the ministry vied to apprentice under him. They chopped his wood and sheared his sheep, and some of them even married his daughters. They all learned the pastoral charge from his example, and they went on to be college presidents and pastors, thus extending his influence throughout the colonies and the young Republic for generations. Such a life yielded many relationships with truly fascinating stories. One writer has used his family as a model for the Christian home, and biographers have turned to his life again and again to challenge audiences for the past three centuries.

Not only is his personal life intriguing, but also he was a prince of pastors. Being a pastor involves two major things: preaching and pastoral care. Edwards excelled at both. His sermons reflect careful attention to the text, acute theological analysis, and precise and graceful application. The Puritans spoke of preaching as the art of prophesying, and Edwards stands as one of this craft's great artists.

He also knew how to pastor. To be sure, he possessed a certain reticence; he was more at home with books than with people, and he largely left the entertaining to Sarah. But he would also take time to visit his parishioners, especially those who, in the words of the Puritans, were "soul anxious." He cared deeply for those under his charge. Even after his removal from Northampton, he carried on quite a correspondence, answering many queries from former congregants.

Edwards also receives much attention from different quarters because he displays the life of the mind. He kept a series of notebooks from his college days until the end of his life. In these notebooks he wrote various thoughts or ideas, some of which are only a few lines long and others that fill pages. In fact, he sometimes returned to certain entries decades later, adding new reflections without skipping a beat. He developed a system of inventive shorthand and cross-referencing that was so elaborate and cryptic that it required military code-breakers to decipher. He had a special writing desk built with multiple drawers and cabinets, keeping particular books in certain drawers. He would then refer to the books by their locations.

These notebooks became the source for sermons, essays, and treatises. One can easily picture Edwards sitting in his study or riding horseback through the Connecticut River Valley ruminating over ideas expressed in his notebooks. These notebooks, called the *Miscellanies,* reveal a life that was consumed by ideas and a life that valued the art of reflection.

Further, Edwards thought about and wrote on a wide variety of topics and issues. He investigated the nature and activity of the flying spider, plumbed the depths of Scripture, explored the contours of ethics, and wrestled with questions of theology. Today scholars from the fields of literature, history, and philosophy, as well as theologians, pastors, and laity, all study and read Jonathan Edwards. Every one of his major treatises is extant well over two hundred years after first appearing in print.

Finally, Edwards stands as a perennial figure and captures the attention of many because of his wholistic devotion to God. In Edwards one sees the whole person—heart, soul, mind, and strength—devoted to God. It is rather fashionable today to pit the head against the heart, and the head usually loses. Such a polarity is foreign to Edwards. He not only makes room for both, but also argues for their necessary mutual existence. This whole devotion was not short-lived, but rather manifested itself throughout his entire life.

I once attended an Edwards conference that ended with a panel discussion. The members of the panel had all worked on Edwards manuscripts, some for decades. Someone in the audience asked the panelists what they had learned from Edwards. I will never forget the words of one panelist, George S. Claghorn. For fifty years Claghorn had been collecting and editing Edwards's letters and personal writings, and he probably knows more about Edwards than anyone. His answer was brief, although memorable and worth repeating: he said Edwards was focused, fearless, and faithful.

A deep sense of the beauty and excellency of God permeates all of Edwards's life and writings. It set his mind on fire and his heart aflame. It is no wonder that he continues to have something to say to the church centuries after his death. And it is no wonder that people continue to listen.

In the chapters that follow we will explore this life as we examine Edwards's thought and writings. First, we will expand on some things mentioned here, sketching out the details of his life in a brief biography. We will look at his early years, his time at Northampton, and the final years at Stockbridge and then Princeton. Key events, such as the Great Awakening, will be our focus as we analyze the impact of these events on his life. The next ten chapters will each explore one of Edwards's writings. Many of the familiar and some of the not-so-familiar texts will be introduced, summarized, and explained. I have also included selections from these texts so you can get a flavor of his writing. The selections break down into three sections exploring the variety of Edwards's works.

In part 2, the first of these three sections, we look at Edwards as a churchman and revivalist, examining his involvement in the Great Awakening and his thought on issues that have an impact on the life of the church. The first text, one of his well-known sermons entitled "God Glorified in the Work of Redemption," sets the stage for this section. Sermons like this one emphasize the great Puritan doctrine of divine sovereignty by stressing humanity's absolute dependence on God in redemption. Such sermons as this one led to the revivals in Northampton and the Great Awakening.

Next follows *A Faithful Narrative*, which recounts the events of a revival in Edwards's own congregation that preceded the Great Awakening. *Religious Affections*, written after the Great Awakening, offers his mature thoughts on the question that surfaced during the revivals: How does one know if a religious conversion, or any religious experience for that matter, is genuine? This section ends with *An Hum-*

*ble Inquiry,* a text on the Lord's Supper, which happened to be the issue surrounding Edwards's dismissal from Northampton.

Part 3 covers various theological and philosophical studies. Texts here examine God's work in and plan for the world, the nature of virtue or ethics, general revelation, and human nature and the will. Two of these texts were published either in Edwards's lifetime or shortly after his death and represent thoughtful and provocative treatments of difficult issues. *History of the Work of Redemption* consists of thirty sermons, in typical Puritan fashion, on one text, Isaiah 51:8. Of course, Edwards brings much more into the sermon than this one text. In fact, he uses this text as an occasion to discuss the whole of Scripture and God's plan for the world. We will focus on the first and last sermons of the series. Next follows "The Wisdom of God in the Contrivance of the World," which comes from one of his notebooks mentioned above. I have paired this writing with his famous "Spider Letter." Here we see Edwards's mind investigating the book of nature as keenly as it explores the book of Scripture.

The final text in this section, *Freedom of the Will,* earned Edwards a transatlantic reputation as a brilliant and formidable defender of Calvinism. The issues raised in this text, such as human responsibility and divine sovereignty, confound theologians and laity alike. While this text is challenging, it is also rather rewarding.

The final section, part 4, again finds Edwards in the pulpit. Three sermons provide us with a sampling of what it would have been like to be a member of his church. The first sermon examined here, "Sinners in the Hands of an Angry God," is Edwards's most famous. For some, this is all they ever will read by Edwards and they usually do not go looking for more. Anthologized in almost every American literature textbook, this is probably the most read sermon of all time. It may also be the most misread sermon of all time and the most misunderstood of Edwards's writings. Consequently, in spite of—or perhaps because of—its familiarity, it provides a good place to begin considering Edwards's preaching. The next sermon, "The Most High, a Prayer-Hearing God," which is not so well known as "Sinners," remarkably portrays Edwards's acute sense of applying Scripture and theology to the Christian life. Prayer remains somewhat of a mystery for many Christians, and through Edwards we can gain valuable insight into this enigmatic but essential discipline.

Finally, we will study the concluding sermon from Edwards's series on 1 Corinthians 13, *Charity and Its Fruits*. While most have the image of Edwards as a preacher of only fire and brimstone, I want you to see another dimension to Edwards as embodied in this sermon, "Heaven Is a World of Love." Here we see Edwards anticipating and celebrating the glorious redemption of God's elect in the consummation of his plan for the world. Edwards found this remarkable idea a source of sheer delight and intense hope that can be contagious to his readers.

This book concludes with a brief guide to various editions of primary texts of Edwards and to a few beneficial secondary works. The ideal introduction to Edwards would devote one chapter to each of his texts, but this would be difficult for writer and reader alike. Texts like *Original Sin, Concerning the End for Which God Created the World, Distinguishing Marks,* and *Some Thoughts Concerning the Present Revival,* as well as many sermons like "A Divine and Supernatural Light," are all worthy of inclusion. Not wanting to try the reader's patience, I have decided to deal with only the ten or so texts and sermons in these chapters. Again, this work is not an end in itself, but a gateway into the rich and rewarding life, thought, and writings of Jonathan Edwards. The conclusion offers you some directions for continuing your journey.

The year 2003 marks the tricentennial of Edwards's birth. With the passing decades and centuries Edwards continues to hold his place as America's foremost theologian, endearing himself to every new generation of the church. My hope is that this book will help you to see the relevance and importance of Edwards's thought and that through these pages Edwards will help you, as he has helped so many others, to better understand God, his Word, his work in this world, and your place in it.

# THE PERSONAL EDWARDS

Much of what we know about Edwards's life comes from his own hand in such writings as his *Resolutions,* diary, "Personal Narrative," and letters. In part 1 we use these writings to explore the various episodes of his life. This part also provides the larger context of the writings examined in later chapters. We begin our tour with Edwards's early years in East Windsor, Connecticut. The parsonage at East Windsor proved quite a training ground for the young scholar and pastor-to-be, and it prepared him well for his collegiate studies. Edwards received his bachelor's degree from Yale, stayed on to receive a master's degree, and then continued for two more years as a tutor.

His time at Yale was interrupted by a brief pastorate in New York City. In 1727 Edwards became an assistant minister at Northampton, Massachusetts, and he married Sarah Pierrepont, who became his lifelong companion. Northampton was home for the Edwards family until 1750. During his stay, his congregation experienced a number of revivals and the colonies enjoyed the Great Awakening. Edwards next moved to the frontier town of Stockbridge, Massachusetts, ministering to Mohicans and Mohawks. He also wrote a number of treatises during his seven-year stay. At the end of 1757, the trustees of the college at Princeton invited him to become president. Edwards took office in January and served until his untimely death on March 22, 1758.

# 1

# A FIRM FOUNDATION

## *The Early Years*

Capturing Jonathan Edwards's life in two brief chapters is somewhat like representing a grand mountain range with only a few pictures. In either case you get only a sampling, and many details are necessarily excluded. Nevertheless, you can still get a reasonably good idea. Our few pictures will consist of key events in Edwards's life that shaped his thinking.

In many ways his life presents a portrait in miniature of colonial American history. The key events of the eighteenth century, including the Seven Years War and the Great Awakening, touched his life. His forebears were among the first settlers, and his descendants were among the leaders of the young Republic. In fact, Edwards's legacy is far-reaching both backward and forward. His great-grandfather came to the colonies as an eighteen-year-old along with Thomas Hooker and the settlers of Hartford, Connecticut, in 1636. Jonathan's father, Harvard-trained clergyman Timothy Edwards, settled in East Windsor, Connecticut, along with his young bride, Esther Stoddard.

## An Education at East Windsor

Timothy came from modest means, while Esther hailed from one of the most prominent families in Connecticut, if not in all of New England. Her father was the acclaimed "Pope of the Connecticut River Valley," Solomon Stoddard, a significant factor in Jonathan's life. Such was Stoddard's influence and prestige that, according to some reports, the difficult road connecting the central Connecticut River Valley to Boston was widened, smoothed over, and turned into an early version of a highway primarily to make it easier for the aging Stoddard to attend significant events in Boston—and especially commencements at Harvard.

Together Timothy and Esther made quite a home for their ten daughters and one son. The family made an impression as all of the children were unusually tall for the day. Neighbors and friends would commonly refer to Timothy and Esther's "60 feet of daughters." As was customary for colonial ministers, Timothy provided the equivalent of grammar school and secondary education for the town's children. This supplemented Timothy's income, as well as provided Jonathan and his sisters the opportunity to grow up among books, learning, and languages.

Sereno E. Dwight's memoir of Jonathan Edwards notes that Timothy's education of his daughters was rather enlightened for the time. All were sent to Boston for finishing school, and the elder daughters assisted their younger brother in his studies. Dwight records a letter Timothy wrote to Esther while serving as a chaplain during an Indian war in 1711. He expresses his wishes that the children be diligent in executing their Latin studies and that Jonathan "continue to recite his Latin to his elder sisters."

Additionally, Jonathan learned Scripture, the catechism, and the rich heritage of the Puritan and Reformed faith from both his father and mother. Again, Dwight records that "Mrs. Edwards was always fond of books, and discovered a very fond acquaintance with them in her conversation; particularly with the best theological writers."

Jonathan also received an education in pastoral ministry from his father. Timothy's sixty-one years as pastor of the congregation of East Windsor provided many hills and valleys from which Edwards could view all angles of shepherding a flock. Although he published only one sermon in his lifetime, Timothy had earned a reputation as a captivating preacher. One scholar has said that Timothy Edwards and Solomon Stoddard provided for Jonathan the "Connecticut River Valley school of preaching." As a student in this school, he observed pulpit orators at work and began to hone his own preaching skills.

Jonathan further witnessed the seasons of revival among his father's congregation. At the age of thirteen, Jonathan wrote to his sister Mary that "through the wonderful mercy and goodness of God there hath in this place been a very remarkable stirring and pouring out of the Spirit of God, and likewise now is, but I think I have reason to think that it is in some measure diminished, but I hope not much. About thirteen have been joined to the church in a state of full communion."

This letter foreshadows two of the most significant features that will figure prominently in Edwards's own future ministry at Northampton: revivals and communion qualifications. There were also disappointments, struggles, and conflicts for the young Jonathan to observe as well. In 1694 the congregation at East Windsor outgrew its building, and a sharp disagreement arose as to the exact location of the new meetinghouse. Twenty years later they finished the new building in an agreeable location.

Further, Timothy, like all New England Congregational ministers, was precariously placed. On the one hand, he was responsible for the spiritual condition of the people, which at times involved church discipline. On the other, both his salary and, for that matter, his very presence in the church were contingent on the congregation's vote. Such a dynamic led the famous Boston minister Increase Mather to say that "the Congregational Church discipline is not suited for a worldly interest or for a formal generation of professors." At East Windsor Jonathan observed his father negotiate the various challenges associated with Congregationalism, challenges Jonathan would face in Northampton.

## Learned and Orthodox Men

By the time Jonathan was ready for college in 1716, Harvard's commitment to the Puritan and Reformed tradition was suspect. So Timothy enrolled his son in the fledgling Collegiate School of Connecticut, which later became Yale University. The college moved around Connecticut until 1719, when it made a permanent home in New Haven. The foundation Edwards began to build in his East Windsor home grew stronger and deeper at Yale. In his bachelor's program he studied the belles-lettres, mastering grammar, rhetoric, logic, ancient history, arithmetic, geometry, and astronomy, as well as metaphysics, ethics, and natural science.

We get a glimpse into his studies in a letter he wrote to his father just prior to his final year as an undergraduate. "I have inquired of Mr. Cutler what books we should have need of the next year," Jonathan writes. "He answered that he would have me get against that time Alsted's *Geometry,* and Gassendi's *Astronomy;* with which I would entreat you to get a pair of dividers or mathematician's compasses, and a scale which are absolutely necessary to learning mathe-

---

FIG. 1.1

---

**The Yale Charter (1701)**

*By the Governor, Council & Representatives of his Majesty's Colony of Connecticut in General Court assembled,*

*New Haven, Oct. 9, 1701:*

*An act for liberty to erect a collegiate school.*

Whereas several well disposed, and publick spiritual persons of their sincere regard to & zeal for upholding & propagating of the Christian Protestant religion by a succession of learned & orthodox men have expressed by petition their earnest desires that full liberty and privilege be granted unto certain undertakers for the founding, suitably endowing & ordering of a collegiate school within his Majesty's Colony of Connecticut wherein youth may be instructed in the arts and sciences who through the blessing of Almighty God may be fitted for publick employment both in church and civil state.

---

matics." This letter also reflects that little has changed since colonial days, as Jonathan ends with a postscript informing his father of the weekly cost of board, a not-so-subtle hint to send money.

Jonathan additionally studied Greek and Hebrew in order to read the biblical text in its original languages as well as the classical Greek texts of literature and philosophy. And of course he embarked on a rigorous course of theology. Not wanting students to neglect the Sabbath or lose sight of their spiritual formation, the Collegiate School faculty and principals required students to take copious notes on sermons given during the Lord's Day. Quizzes would then be given that week on the sermons to ensure that students had paid attention.

In forming their schools, the Puritans in New England copied perfectly the curricula of Oxford and Cambridge from Old England and provided a true liberal arts education. Far from being vocational training for a profession, the B.A. degree served only to produce educated gentlemen. The professional training necessary to become a minister, lawyer, physician, or merchant came through apprenticeships after graduation.

Yale also exposed young Edwards to the so-called new learning and the works of Isaac Newton and John Locke. He further became poignantly aware of the writings of deists, who claimed Newton's work demonstrates that God's involvement with his creation is unnecessary. The mechanical universe, which God "wound up," works quite fine on its own. It even, they argued, precludes any interference by God. This amounts to disclaiming the possibility of miracles and to elevating general revelation over Scripture—if not doing away with Scripture altogether.

Edwards saw things differently. He discerned in Newton's work the marvelous presence and intimate involvement of God in this world. Far from pointing to God's absence, Newton's work enabled Edwards to see the absolute necessity of God's actively sustaining his creation. Newton's impact on Edwards is seen in his various scientific essays, such as "The Wisdom of God in the Contrivance of the World." Edwards also utilized Newton indirectly in writings that exposed the errors of deism. Edwards feared that deism might overtake the church. History has proven those fears to have been well founded, as many formerly orthodox Congregational churches in New England turned to Unitarianism in the nineteenth century.

Edwards's relationship to the work of John Locke is a bit more complex. The late Perry Miller went so far as to say that Edwards's reading of Locke's *Essay Concerning Human Understanding* was the central and defining moment in his entire life. Some, such as Iain H. Murray, have said this claim is exaggerated. Nonetheless, Edwards did in fact read thoroughly and consider Locke's ideas in *Essay*. Much of Edwards's interest centers around Locke's theory of knowledge, which may be referred to as empiricism, or, as Locke preferred, sensationalism. This theory holds that all of one's knowledge comes through the senses or experience.

Locke's epistemology also emphasizes that knowledge consists of ideas. Of particular interest here is Edwards's understanding of the "new sense," which figures prominently in his writings. His reading of Locke also probably prompted his discussion of "affections." Edwards treats both the new sense and the affections at length in his *Treatise Concerning Religious Affections*.

At the same time Edwards read Newton and Locke, he continued to explore his Puritan and Reformed heritage. John Calvin, John Owen, William Ames, and others surfaced repeatedly throughout his Yale education. In fact, like his other colleagues, Edwards set about the task of memorizing Ames's *Marrow of Theology*. At any time an upperclassman could call upon his younger cohort to recite a certain section from *Marrow*. If the student lapsed at this critical moment, then he was met with kitchen duty for the week. A powerful incentive, to be sure, to keep up with one's studies.

Edwards's study of and devotion to Calvinism also alerted him to the errors of Arminianism and the inroads it was making among New England theologians and churches. Much of his writing and preaching focused on these errors in an attempt to stem the tide of Arminianism's influence. We will especially see his mind at work on these issues in the sermon "God Glorified in the Work of Redemption" and his treatise *Freedom of the Will.*

Edwards successfully navigated Yale's curriculum and received his B.A. in 1720, graduating at the top of his class. He stayed at Yale as a student in the master's program from 1720 to 1722. One incident that reveals life at Yale was not about books and learning exclusively concerns a student rebellion over the food served in the commons. Again Jonathan records the incident in a letter to his father. The students banded together in protest and boycotted a meal. Edwards is sympathetic with his classmates to a point, but thinks they have gone too far. "I must needs say for my own part, that although the commons at sometimes have not been sufficient as to quality," he writes, "yet I think there has been very little occasion for such an insurrection as this."

**The Altering of Appearances**

The year 1721 also marks the conversion of Jonathan Edwards. His conversion at a relatively late date and after so much exposure to the gospel might come as a surprise to contemporary audiences. It reflects, however, the tendencies of the day. Perhaps the Puritan's most feared enemy was self-deception or hypocrisy in matters of religion. Consequently, claiming conversion or conversion itself was not something anyone in those days took lightly.

In fact, Edwards's own mother did not receive communion at her husband's church until well into her adult years. In Edwards's case he did not experience God's work of conversion until his second year of graduate studies at Yale. One of his most endearing writings, the so-called "Personal Narrative" (see fig. 1.2), which was probably written in 1734 as

FIG. 1.2

**"Personal Narrative" (1734?)**

After [my conversion] my sense of divine things gradually increased, and became more and more lively, and had more of that inward sweetness. The appearance of everything was altered: there seemed to be as it were a calm, sweet cast, or appearance of divine glory, in almost everything. God's excellency, his wisdom, his purity and love, seemed to appear in everything; in the sun, moon and stars; in the clouds and blue sky; in the grass, flowers, trees; in the water, and all nature; which used greatly to fix my mind. I often used to sit and view the moon, for a long time; and so in the daytime, spent much time in viewing the clouds and sky, to behold the sweet glory of God in these things: in the meantime, singing forth with a low voice, my contemplations of the Creator and Redeemer. . . .

I have loved the doctrines of the Gospel: they have been to my soul like green pastures. The gospel has seemed to me to be the richest treasure; the treasure that I have most desired, and longed that it might dwell richly in me. The way of salvation by Christ, has appeared in a general way, glorious and excellent, and most pleasant and beautiful. It has often seemed to me, that it would in great measure spoil heaven, to receive it in any other way.

Edwards looked back on his conversion, vividly portrays the transformation that overcame him as the Triune God opened his eyes to the glorious gospel and gave him, in his words, that new sense of divine things.

Between his years studying in the master's program and completing his thesis, he briefly pastored a Presbyterian church in the young city of New York. Somewhere in the vicinity of Broadway and Wall Street, Edwards ministered for ten months. The congregation he ministered to was the result of a church split. Edwards came in August 1722, and by April 1723, due in large part to Edwards's persuasion, the small congregation decided to reunite with the church they had left. While ministering to that small assembly, he began exploring, in meticulously prepared sermons, many of the themes that would dominate his later preaching and writing.

## Disciplines of a Godly Thinker

Edwards wrote not only sermons, but also other kinds of works, including his *Resolutions.* Numbering seventy in all, these resolutions were intended to serve as a guide to his life. They begin with a humble acknowledgment of dependence on God: "Being sensible that I am unable to do anything without God's help, I do humbly entreat him by his grace to enable me to keep these Resolutions, so far as they are agreeable to his will, for Christ's sake." Here is just a sampling of these commitments:

1.  Resolved, that I will do whatsoever I think to be the most to God's glory, and my own good, profit, and pleasure in the whole of my duration, without any consideration of the time, whether now, or never so many myriads of ages hence. Resolved to do what-

soever I think to be my duty, and most for the good and advantage of mankind in general. Resolved to do this, whatever difficulties I meet with, how many and how great soever.

6. Resolved, to live with all my might, while I do live.

20. Resolved, to maintain the strictest temperance in eating and drinking.

52. I frequently hear persons in old age say how they would live, if they were to live their lives over again: resolved, that I will live just so as I can think I shall wish I had done, supposing I live to old age.

56. Resolved, never to give over, nor in the least to slacken my fight with my corruptions, however unsuccessful I may be.

67. Resolved, after afflictions, to inquire, what I am the better for them, what good I have got by them, and what I might have gotten by them.

70. Let there be something of benevolence in all that I speak.

He prefaced these resolutions with this note: "Remember to read over these Resolutions once a week."

In addition to the *Resolutions,* Edwards started a diary that he intermittently kept from 1722 to 1725 and then added just four entries in 1734 and 1735. Keeping a diary was a typical Puritan practice, serving much like an X-ray of the soul. It enabled them to face and hopefully keep at bay that dreaded enemy of self-deception. Edwards's diary reflects moments of both triumph and defeat. On January 2, 1723, he begins his diary entry with the word *dull,* then on the 9th he begins with *decayed,* and by the 10th he writes "Reviving." These early entries in the diary also reflect the content of the *Resolutions* and record his attempts at keeping them. The following excerpts from his diary are typical:

> Friday night, Oct. 12 [1723]. I see there are some things quite contrary to the soundness and perfection of Christianity, in which almost all good men do allow themselves, and where innate corruption has an unrestrained secret vent, which they never take notice of, or think to be no hurt, or cloak under the name of virtue; which things exceedingly darken the brightness, and hide the loveliness, of Christianity. Who can understand his errors? O that I might be kept from secret faults!

> Monday January 20, [1724]. I have been very much to blame, in that I have not been as full, and plain and downright, in my standing up for virtue and religion, when I have had fair occasion, before those who seemed to take no delight in such things. If such conversation would not be agreeable to them, I have in some degree minced the matter, that I might not displease, and might not speak right against the grain, more than I should have loved to have done with others, to whom it would be agreeable to speak directly for religion. I ought to be exceedingly bold with such persons, not talking in a melancholy strain, but in one confident and fearless, assured of the truth and excellence of the cause.

Edwards started another writing project during this time: his most curious and intriguing *Miscellanies*. These writings, varying from one-sentence thoughts to pages-long reflections, were arranged in eight volumes by Edwards and then carefully indexed in a ninth volume. Sometimes he pulled out of the *Miscellanies* a single entry and devoted a new notebook to expounding that one thought. The *Miscellanies* involves everything from philosophical and scientific explorations to exegetical notes on a biblical passage, from the authorship of Genesis to the nature of vision.

He entered the first installment in the *Miscellanies* in 1722 and continued adding to this work throughout his life. These ideas became the source of many sermons, and some of the ideas eventually saw publication in his treatises. Near the end of his life, he explained his methodology in the *Miscel-*

The Edwards Memorial. A life-size bronze plaque mounted at First Church, Northampton. Sculpted by Herbert Adams.

*lanies* in a letter to Princeton's trustees, in response to their invitation to become the school's president:

> My method of study, from my first beginning the work of ministry, has been very much by writing; applying myself in this way, to improve every important hint; pursuing the clue to my utmost, when anything in reading, meditation or conversation, has been suggested to my mind, that seemed to promise light in any weighty point. Thus penning what appeared to me my best thoughts, on innumerable subjects for my own benefit. The longer I prosecuted my studies in this method, the more habitual it became, and the more pleasant and profitable I found it.

The *Miscellanies* were his constant companion. Even during his daily exercise routine of horseback riding, Edwards turned over ideas in his mind. In more pleasant weather he would carry along ink and paper, stop in a meadow or near a stream, and sketch a few lines.

The cold months disallowed writing outdoors, so Edwards developed the habit of pinning pieces of cloth to his coat, associating the cloth with a particular idea. When he returned to his study he removed the cloth, remembered the idea, and recorded it. This practice also proved helpful on long journeys. This peculiar habit was quite the talk around town, and neighbors always knew he had been on a long journey when he rode in covered with pieces of cloth. Writing *Miscellanies* proved a lifelong profession and passion, revealing that Edwards's mind was constantly at work.

## Completing the Foundation

In April 1723 Jonathan returned to Connecticut. He provided pulpit supply for various churches throughout New England, and he wrote his master's thesis. He received the

The manuscript of Edwards's master's thesis consists of nine pages and measures 4.5" x 6". The thesis is an original composition in Latin and concerns the doctrine of imputation.

M.A. at Yale's graduation in September 1723. Today graduations are rather perfunctory events. They occur after the student has completed all of his or her work, making the ceremony itself a formality. Commencements were more dramatic in colonial days: each candidate was required to present his master's thesis—in Latin—before the audience and faculty, and then to defend it—in Latin—in order to receive his degree.

Consequently commencements were quite entertaining and typically drew large crowds. They served as colonial New England's version of the Superbowl. Edwards argued in his thesis that the only means by which a sinner can be justified before God is the righteousness of Christ. His thesis presents a remarkably concise, yet definitive argument for the Reformation doctrine of imputation, both of Adam's sin and of Christ's righteousness. It was quite well received by faculty and audience alike, who knew that this was only the beginning for this young but articulate and formidable theologian.

Following graduation Edwards tried his hand at writing in a different genre by drafting an essay on the flying spider. At the urging of his father, he addressed a letter to Judge Paul Dudley, a friend of his father and also a Fellow of the Royal Society of London. Tradition had Edwards writing the famous "Spider Letter" as a mere twelve-year-old. We know now that he actually wrote it in October 1723. Edwards hoped that his essay would find its way into publication in the transactions of the Royal Society.

He also returned to the pulpit and served the Congregational church in Bolton, Connecticut, as essentially an interim pastor at the end of 1723. By the spring of 1724, however, Edwards returned to Yale as a tutor (or instructor), a post he would hold for two years.

Edwards's early writings—his master's thesis, the "Spider Letter," and his sermons—testify to his numerous gifts. He had abilities in the natural sciences, the necessary training and skills as a theologian, and experience and dexterity in the pulpit. Edwards lacked neither talent nor opportunity. But he had only one life, and perhaps during these two years he reflected on his options, discerned the direction he should go, and simultaneously grew personally, intellectually, and spiritually.

These early writings also point to the diversity of Edwards's interests. Those who study him sometimes portray him as either a philosopher or a theologian, or they view him as one with an academic bent versus one with an inclination to the ministry. This leads them to conclude that his time as a tutor at Yale, such writings as the essay on the flying spider, and his philosophical inquiries were misdirected. Others lament the loss of Edwards to the intellectual history of America when he stepped into the pulpit.

Such polarities, however, would probably amuse Edwards. Far from being schizophrenic, he saw the value in all of these endeavors, allowing his philosophical and scientific training and activity, and his exegetical skills and theological heritage, to mutually inform each other. A diary entry reveals his tendency to move between issues of divinity and philosophy without seeing any conflict:

> Thursday, Feb 6 [1724]. More convinced than ever of the usefulness of a free religious conversation. I find that while conversing on natural philosophy, I gain knowledge abundantly faster, and see the reasons of things much clearer, than in private study. Wherefore, earnestly to seek at all times for religious conversation; for those that I can with profit and delight and freedom so converse with.

Nevertheless, Edwards had a choice to make concerning his life's work. While excelling in academia, he spent the majority of his life in the church. His early years at the East Windsor parsonage, Yale, and New York, as well as the personal disciplines he cultivated, all contributed to establishing a firm foundation that Edwards built on during his life of ministry. And he began this new period of his life at Northampton.

*2*

---

# A SINGULAR DEVOTION

*The Later Years*

J onathan Edwards, wasting no time in building on the foundation of his early years, answered a call to serve as the assistant minister in Northampton, Massachusetts. This town might sound familiar: it was the home of Jonathan's mother. Her father, Solomon Stoddard, had been pastor since 1669 of this church, located in the center of Massachusetts. The congregation decided that Stoddard needed an assistant, whom the senior minister would groom to succeed him. Edwards would spend the majority of his adult life in this active town, located in the heart of the Connecticut River Valley.

## The Lady from New Haven

Edwards officially became assistant minister in the church in 1727. This was a banner year for Edwards, as he married Sarah Pierrepont on July 28. Sarah first captured Jonathan's attention during his student years. She was only thirteen then, and he had just returned from New York City. He was so enraptured by her that on a blank leaf in a book he was reading he wrote an inscription memorializing her spiritual character (see fig. 2.1).

Presumably they began a long courtship, marrying four years later. Together they had eight daughters and three sons. Jonathan and Sarah enjoyed a close relationship with all of their children—no small task given the size of the family and the pressures their famous father constantly felt. Although he coveted his daily time in his study, Jonathan also devoted time to his children in the morning for devotions, at meals, and during evenings. His letters to them not only re-

---

FIG. 2.1

**"On Sarah Pierrepont" (1723)**

They say there is a young lady in New Haven who is beloved of the Great Being who made and rules the world, and that there are certain seasons in which this Almighty Being, in some way or other invisible, comes to her and fills her mind with exceeding sweet delight, and that she hardly cares for any thing, except to meditate on him. . . .

She is of wonderful sweetness, calmness, and universal benevolence of mind; especially after this Great God has manifested himself to her mind. She will sometimes go about from place to place, singing sweetly; and seems to be always full of joy and pleasure; and no one knows for what. She loves to be alone, walking in the fields and groves, and seems to have someone invisible always conversing with her.

---

flect his love and concern for them, but also offer a glimpse into colonial life.

Two letters to his daughter Esther are especially intriguing. The first letter, written in Northampton on November 3, 1746, relays information concerning the family's safety during French and Indian battles. It was sent to Esther while she and her older sister, Sarah, were visiting family friends in Long Island.

Dear Child,

We are all through mercy in a tolerable state of health. Our house is now forted in, and a watch is kept here every night in the fort, but there has been no mischief done by the enemy in this country, since the taking of Massachusetts Fort. I am ready to think that the French and Indians have lately turned their course another way, down towards Annapolis [Nova Scotia], to join the French fleet. . . .

We all give our love to you and Sarah. . . . I would not have you be discouraged and melancholy, though you are far from home; God is everywhere, and I hope you will walk closely with him, and will have much of his presence. Your circumstances in East Hampton are on some accounts more comfortable than your sisters at home, for you lie down and rise and have none to make you afraid. Here we have been in much fear of an army suddenly rushing in upon the town in the night to destroy it. We daily remember you in our prayers to God, who I hope will be with you continually and will in every respect be gracious to you. I am, my dear child,

Your affectionate father,
Jonathan Edwards

Another letter, written in Stockbridge on March 28, 1753, offers some rather curious potions for Esther's infirmities shortly after she moved to Princeton and married

Aaron Burr. Jonathan first reflects on God's purpose for suffering in her life and reminds her of her ultimate goal. He then offers his remedies.

Dear Child,

We are glad to hear that you are in any respect better, but concerned at your remaining great weakness. I am glad to see some of the contents of your letter to your mother; and particularly that you have been enabled to make a free-will offering of yourself to God's service, and that you have experienced some inward divine consolations under your affliction, by the extreme weakness and distressing pains, you have been the subject of. For these you ought to be thankful, and also for that unwearied kindness and tender care of your companion [Aaron Burr], which you speak of. I would not have you think that any strange thing has happened to you in this affliction; 'tis according to the course of things in this world, that after the world's smiles, some great affliction soon comes. . . . You are like to spend the rest of your life at a great distance from your parents; but care not much for that. If you lived near us, yet our breath and yours would soon go forth, and we should return to our dust, whither we are all hastening. 'Tis of infinitely more importance to have the presence of an heavenly Father and to make progress towards an heavenly home. Let us all take care that we may meet there at last.

As to means for your health, we have procured one rattlesnake, which is all we could get. It is a medicine that has been very serviceable to you heretofore, and I would have you try it still. If your stomach is very weak and will bear but little, you must take it in smaller quantities. We have sent you some ginseng. I should think it best for you to make trial of that various ways: try stewing it in water, and take it in strength and quantity as you find suits your stomach best. You may also try steeping it in wine, in good Madeira or Claret; or if these wines are too harsh then in some good white wine. . . . And above all the rest, use riding in pleasant weather; and when you can bear it, riding on horseback; but never so as to fatigue you. And be very careful to avoid taking cold. And I should think it best pretty much to throw by doctors, and be your own physician, hearkening to them that are used to your constitution.

I desire that Mr. Burr and you would be frequent in counseling [your brother] Timmy as to his soul-concerns.

Commending you to God, before whom we daily remember you in our prayers, I am

Your affectionate father,
Jonathan Edwards

P.S. Your mother would have you use a conserve of raisins; a pound of good sugar to a pound of raisins, after they are stoned. . . . Your mother also has an inclination that you should sometimes try a tea made of the leaves of Robin's plantain, if it be known at Newark by that name; she says she has found it very strengthening and comfortable to her in her weakness. The family all unites in their love to you.

One can only imagine Esther's surprise upon receiving that rattlesnake. In this letter Edwards also requests that Esther and her husband look after her younger brother Timothy. Timothy was a student at Princeton, and a letter to him further reveals Jonathan as a caring parent; enclosed were money and a new pair of stockings. He reminds his son that it has been awhile since he has written, and he asks for an update on his studies and events at Princeton.

One final letter, written in Northampton on June 22, 1748, was addressed to Sarah while she was traveling to Boston. During her absence, Jonathan's Uncle John Stoddard passed away, and the exact time of her return to Northampton is uncertain. Jonathan deeply misses her, especially because he has a house full of sick children. He also asks her to bring back from Boston some good cheese.

> My Dear Companion,
>
> I wrote you a few lines the last sabbath day by Ensign [Timothy] Dwight, which I hope you will receive. By this I will inform you that [our daughter] Betty seems really to be on the mending hand. I can't but think she is truly better, both as to her health and her sores, since she has been at Mrs. Phelp's. The first two or three days, before she was well acquainted, she was very unquiet; but now more quiet than she used to be at home. This is lecture-day morning and your two eldest daughters went to bed last night, both sick, and rose beat out and having the headache. . . . How Sarah [and] Esther do today I can't tell, for they are not up. We have been without you almost as long as we know how to be, but yet are willing you should obey the calls of providence with regard to Col. Stoddard.
>
> If you have money to spare, and it ben't too late, I should be glad if you would buy us some cheese in Boston and [send it] with other things if it can be safely. . . .
>
> I am your most affectionate companion,
> Jonathan Edwards

Edwards's example in his personal life rivals his example as a pastor, theologian, and philosopher. He loved his wife and his children, and the legacy of his descendants stands as a testimony to his devotion. Jonathan and Sarah were united in a single desire to see each other and their eleven children walking closely with God and, as he wrote to Esther, meeting in heaven at last.

His daughters married lawyers, a politician, and a minister who became a college president. One son was a lawyer, another was a politician, and another was a minister and a college president. Edwards had seventy-two grandchildren, although he did not live long enough to see many of them. His descendants are so numerous and played such significant roles that their removal might possibly have changed the course of American history.

## Years of Surprise at Northampton

Due to Solomon Stoddard's untimely death in 1729, Edwards suddenly found himself in one of the most prestigious and influential pulpits in New England before his twenty-seventh birthday. He continued his practice of meticulously preparing his sermon manuscripts during his early years at Northampton. Sometimes he would write out one sermon numerous times, constantly reworking whole sections and even phrases until he got it just right. He would then manufacture a booklet out of the manuscript by folding the leaves and sewing them together.

He also continued writing in his notebooks and began his own commentary on the Bible in his *Blank Bible*. This Bible, a gift from his brother-in-law, contained approximately nine hundred interleaved blank pages. Edwards used these blank pages to write his own commentary on a large majority of scriptural passages. He used the *Blank Bible* along with his *Miscellanies* as a source of ideas for sermons. He did not always continue the practice of writing out his sermons. Especially during busy times, his sermon manuscripts consisted of outlines and phrases. Pastors today may be encouraged to learn that he sometimes repreached sermons delivered previously and often borrowed portions from former sermons and inserted them into new ones.

In 1731 Edwards was thrust into the spotlight: he was invited to give the Thursday lecture before a crowd of clergy in Boston. This practice extended back to the days of the settling of Massachusetts. It provided a means to minister to fellow ministers and enabled them to learn from each other. For the one in the pulpit, however, this situation could be intimidating.

Edwards especially was under the microscope. First, he was under pressure to match his predecessor's ability in the pulpit. Second, as an alumnus of Yale, he did not share the Harvard credentials of most of the audience. Finally, the growing Arminian threat hung over the gathering, and the clergy assembled were probably anxious to hear Jonathan's thoughts on the subject. His sermon, "God Glorified in the Work of Redemption," exceeded every challenge and was so appreciated by the audience that they saw to its publication.

A few years later revivals began in his congregation at Northampton and some surrounding towns. Many in the town were converted as they experienced, in Puritan terms, a season of awakening. Edwards relayed the events in a letter to a fellow minister in Boston, Benjamin Colman. Colman immediately asked Edwards to expand the letter for publication. Jonathan wrote a more detailed account and sent it to Colman, who quickly published it in 1736 as *A Faithful Narrative of the Surprizing Work of God in the Conversion of Many Hundred Souls in Northampton.*

The work found its way to London and into the hands of the famous hymn writer Isaac Watts and a London minister, John Guyse. Watts and Guyse edited and published an edition of *A Faithful Narrative* in 1737, thus giving the colonial Edwards a transatlantic reputation as a writer and minister.

These revivals were only the beginning, a precursor of the Great Awakening in 1740–1742. From the human perspective two people figure prominently in this event: the Awakening's preacher, George Whitefield, and its theologian, Jonathan Edwards. The two spent extended time together, as Whitefield preached two services in Northampton and even held meetings in Edwards's home. Whitefield's ministry there came in response to the following invitation from Edwards, written in Northampton on February 12, 1740:

Sir,

My request to you is that in your intended journey through New England the next summer, you would be pleased to visit Northampton. I hope it is not wholly from curiosity that I desire to see and hear you in this place; but I apprehend, from what I have heard, that you are one that has the blessing of heaven attending you wherever you go; and I have a great desire, if it may be the will of God, that such a blessing as attends your person and labors may descend on this town, and may enter mine own house, and that I may receive it in mine own soul.

Indeed I am fearful whether you will not be disappointed in New England, and have less success here than in other places: we who have dwelt in a land that has been distinguished with light, and have long enjoyed the gospel, and have been glutted with it, and have despised it, are I fear more hardened than most of those places where you have preached hitherto. But yet I hope in that power and mercy of God that has appeared so triumphant in the success of your labors in other places, that he will send a blessing with you even to us, though we are unworthy of it. . . .

I fear that it is too much for me to desire a particular remembrance in your prayers, when I consider how many thousands do doubtless desire it, who can't all be particularly mentioned; and I am far from thinking myself worthy to be distinguished. But pray, Sir, let your heart be lifted to God for me among others, that God would bestow much of that blessed Spirit on me that he has bestowed on you, and make me also an instrument of his glory. I am, reverend Sir,

Unworthy to be called your fellow laborer,
Jonathan Edwards

---

**FIG. 2.2**

---

**Transcription of Letter to Joseph Bellamy (1748)**

Northampton, April 4, 1748

Rev. & Dear Brother,

I here send a couple of bags to put our wool into, to be sent to Hartford to Mr. Potwine's, desiring you to take care of that matter as you have very kindly manifested yourself willing to do. I trust entirely in your friendship and faithfulness in that matter.

You have probably before now heard of our afflictions in the death of our daughter, Jerusha, who died after 5 days illness, Feb 14. I have great satisfaction concerning her state, from what I know of her life, & what appeared in her at death. Mr. [David] Brainerd, who had much intimate acquaintance with her, she having been constantly with him as his nurse, 19 weeks before his death, expressed great satisfaction concerning the state of her soul, & that he looked on her not only as a saint, but as a very eminent saint. I desire your prayers for us, that God would make up our great loss in spiritual blessings.

Please to accept one of my books on prayer for the revival of religion, which I here send you. And send me word whether the proposal for united prayer be complied with in your parts.

I wrote to you some time since informing that I was about to publish Mr. Brainerd's life from his private writings, desiring you to send me any letters of his worthy to be inserted, but have had no answer. I would now renew that request, and also that you would send me word whether you will allow me to mention your name in the printed proposals for subscription, or one that will take in subscriptions in your parts. This with respectful salutations to Mrs. Bellamy, is from Dear Sir,

Your affectionate friend and brother,
Jonathan Edwards

---

To say that Edwards was the theologian of the Awakening is not to suggest that he was a less than formidable preacher. In fact, his preaching of his most famous sermon, "Sinners in the Hands of an Angry God," at Enfield, Connecticut, may have been the high-water mark of the Awakening. But Whitefield's extensive, itinerant preaching up and down the colonies spread the revival beyond the Connecticut River Valley.

---

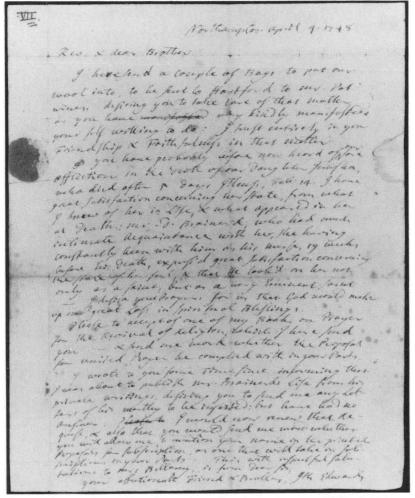

This letter to Joseph Bellamy, dated April 4, 1748, runs the spectrum of Edwards's interests. Beginning with financial matters relating to his sheep, Edwards discusses plans for a concert of prayer, his writings, and his daughter's death. See the transcription opposite.

Edwards's influence came through the quick publication and widespread circulation of his sermons and through his treatises, including *A Faithful Narrative, The Distinguishing Marks of a Work of the Spirit of God* (1741), and *Some Thoughts Concerning the Present Revival* (1742). His *Treatise*

*Concerning Religious Affections* (1746) especially established him as the colonies' theologian.

## Mr. Edwards's School

Edwards did his own share of itinerant preaching throughout Connecticut and Massachusetts. Young ministers customarily invited someone who had influenced them to preach at their installation services. Nearly everyone wanted Jonathan Edwards. His ordination sermons were so numerous that one scholar wrote an entire dissertation on them.

While invitations to ordination services flooded his Northampton home, candidates for the ministry lined up outside his door. Ministerial preparation in those days consisted of both a college education and an apprenticeship. During the 1730s and 1740s Jonathan and Sarah's home was full not only of children, but also of ministerial candidates drawn by Edwards's preaching and writing. Among them were Joseph Bellamy, Samuel Buell, and Samuel Hopkins, all of whom became influential figures in New England.

One other boarder also deserves mention. In the late spring of 1747, a young missionary to Native Americans in New Jersey and Pennsylvania, David Brainerd, paid an extended visit. During the previous winter Brainerd had contracted a serious illness. Jonathan's detailed descriptions of David's symptoms clearly reveal that he suffered from tuberculosis. On October 9, 1747, Brainerd died in Edwards's home. There is a tradition that Jerusha, daughter of Jonathan and Sarah, was engaged to Brainerd, although there is no explicit supporting evidence. Jerusha probably did serve as his nurse during the intense stages of his illness. She contracted tuberculosis as well, and died on February 15, 1748. The two are buried near each other in Northampton.

FIG. 2.4

**Timeline**

| | |
|---|---|
| 1703 | Born on October 5 in East Windsor, Conn. |
| 1716 | Enters Yale. |
| 1720 | Receives B.A. degree from Yale. |
| 1722-23 | Serves pastorate in New York City. |
| 1723 | Writes "Spider Letter" in October. Receives M.A. degree from Yale. |
| 1724-26 | Works as a tutor at Yale. |
| 1727-29 | Serves as assistant minister, Northampton Church. |
| 1727 | Marries Sarah Pierrepont on July 28. |
| 1729-50 | Serves as minister, Northampton Church. |
| 1731 | Writes "God Glorified in the Work of Redemption." |
| 1735 | Writes "The Most High, a Prayer-Hearing God." |
| 1737 | *A Faithful Narrative* is published. |
| 1738 | Preaches series "Charity and Its Fruits" (published in 1851). |
| 1739 | Preaches series "History of the Work of Redemption" (published in 1774). |
| 1740-42 | Instrumental in the Great Awakening. |
| 1741 | Preaches "Sinners in the Hands of an Angry God." |
| 1746 | *Treatise Concerning Religious Affections* is published. |
| 1749 | *An Humble Inquiry Concerning Communion* is published. |
| 1750 | Dismissed by Northampton Church on June 22. |
| 1752-57 | Serves as minister at Indian missionary outpost in Stockbridge, Mass. |
| 1754 | *Freedom of the Will* is published. |
| 1758 | Becomes president of Princeton College. Dies on March 22 in Princeton, N.J. |

Brainerd had kept a diary of his experiences and travels, and he intended to publish it. Knowing that both Brainerd's diary and his remarkable life deserved a public audience, Edwards used the diary as a basis for his biography of the young man he so admired. *An Account of the Life of the Rev. David Brainerd,* first published in Boston in 1749, soon became a best-seller and went through numerous editions and reprintings. In fact, in Edwards's own lifetime this was his most popular work. It continues to be an inspiring missionary biography and an example of a life devoted to the cause of Christ.

Edwards's home was also frequented by children. Many Sunday afternoons he catechized not only his own children but also those of his congregation. He continued the tradition of educating children and preparing them for college.

One story provides what is probably a typical example of Edwards's creativity and patience as a teacher. He tried to explain to a boy that a two-inch cube is eight times as large as a one-inch cube. Having no success, he cut two blocks of wood, one measuring two inches cubed, the other measuring one. He proceeded to cut the first block into eight pieces, all the same size as the one-inch block. As creative as Edwards's demonstration was, the pupil was still not convinced, thinking instead that Edwards had just performed a magic trick. This provides a wonderful picture of a brilliant mind guiding those under his care to comprehend both God's Word and his world.

## June 22, 1750

Like his father's ministry, Edwards's ministry did not consist only of mountaintop experiences. In fact, a bitter conflict with his congregation resulted in his dismissal in 1750. This event may be one of the great mysteries of church history. How can one of America's greatest pastors and its foremost theologian be voted out of his church? To get at the answer we must go back to Edwards's grandfather, Solomon Stoddard. Stoddard had initiated the halfway covenant, which allowed people to partake of communion who, though baptized, had not professed Christ.

In his early ministry Edwards followed this practice, although he had reservations about it. Following the revivals of the mid-1730s and the early 1740s, Edwards noticed that many who had professed Christ trailed off in their commitment to the church. He began to question the genuineness of their religious experiences. In fact, this essentially prompted the sermon series that resulted in his famous *Treatise Concerning Religious Affections*. After weighing the potentially negative impact of the halfway covenant, he did away with it.

This did not sit well with the church's elite, and soon Edwards and his congregation were deeply divided. He sums this up well in a letter to his Scottish friend John Erskine in 1749:

> A very great difficulty has arisen between me and my people, relating to qualifications for communion at the Lord's table. My honored grandfather Stoddard, my predecessor in the ministry over this church, strenuously maintained the Lord's Supper to be a converting ordinance; and urged all to come who were not of scandalous life, though they knew themselves to be unconverted. I formerly conformed to this practice, but I have had difficulties with respect to it, which have been long increasing; till I dared no longer in the former way: which has occasioned great uneasiness among my people, and has filled all the country with noise; which has obliged me to write something on the subject, which is now in the press. I know not but this affair will issue in a separation between me and my people. I desire your prayers that God would guide me in every step in this affair.

The book he mentions is *An Humble Inquiry into the Rules of the Word of God Concerning the Qualifications Requisite to a*

*Compleat Standing and Full Communion in the Visible Christian Church.* It was published in Boston later that year. The elders at Northampton requested that Edwards write this work in defense of his position, but they were not swayed by his arguments. The Northampton Church record notes the outcome of the dispute rather impassively: "June 22, 1750, the Revd Jonathan Edwards was dismissed."

## On the Frontier

Even after being voted out and before being replaced, Edwards continued to preach at Northampton. The church soon found a successor, however, and Edwards went to the frontier town of Stockbridge, Massachusetts, where he began ministering in a missionary outpost to Mohicans and Mohawks. Edwards had exchanged his 400-plus congregation and extremely taxing duties for a small fellowship and a more manageable schedule. Consequently, he again found time to write. During these seven years he penned some of his most noteworthy treatises, including *Freedom of the Will, Original Sin, Concerning the End for Which God Created the World,* and *The Nature of True Virtue.*

This is not to suggest that he neglected his ministerial duties. The mission at Stockbridge received its funds largely from British benefactors desiring to see established not only a thriving church, but also a boarding school for Mohican and Mohawk children. While his predecessor had put little energy into either task, Edwards both preached faithfully and turned his home into a school, providing an excellent education.

Even this ministry, however, was not free from controversy. Tension between the French and Native Americans and the British, which had been brewing for decades and eventuated in the Seven Years War (1756–1763), was felt in any mission work among Native Americans, especially in a frontier town like Stockbridge. Additionally, European settlers did not always treat Native Americans fairly in business deals, which tended to alienate them and made them skeptical of colonists' attempts to help.

Despite these challenges Edwards forged a ministry to the Mohawks, continued his transatlantic correspondence, and wrote several major treatises. Due to his personal discipline, the years from 1750 to 1757, far from being an exile, turned out to be the most productive of his life. If he had stayed at Northampton, would he have been able to devote so much time to writing and leave the literary legacy that he did for generations to come?

In his ministry at both Northampton and Stockbridge, Edwards was no stranger to conflict. He did not seek it out, however, and when it came, he sought resolution in a way that honored truth and justice and glorified God. One diary entry reflects his perspective on handling conflict: "Tuesday, Dec. 31 [1724]. At Night. Concluded never to suffer nor express any angry emotions more or less, except the honor of God calls for it, in zeal for him, or to preserve myself from being trampled on." What he learned then assisted him through the battles he faced later in life.

## President Edwards

Even on the frontier Edwards continued to be one of America's most prominent figures. When the need came for a new president of the College of New Jersey (which later became Princeton University), the trustees of the college chose Edwards. His predecessor was his son-in-law, Aaron Burr Sr., husband of Jonathan's daughter Esther and father of America's third vice-president, Aaron Burr Jr.

These two buildings, which still stand on the Princeton University campus, were the only two buildings of the young college during Edwards's presidency. On the left is Nassau Hall; to the right, the house that served as Edwards's residence. He died in a room on the second floor on March 22, 1758. Original artwork by W. Tennent; engraving by Henry Dawkins, 1764.

In his letter to the trustees, he notes that, though surprised and honored by their offer, he is unsure of accepting it: the move will cause disruption to his family, his own "defects" render him unfit for the office, and he desires to continue his writing projects. Nevertheless, he accepted the invitation, setting out for Princeton in December 1757 and arriving in January 1758.

Edwards's tenure as president, however, was quite short. He volunteered for a smallpox inoculation in part to demonstrate that others need not fear this medical advance. This action also reminds us of Edwards's inquisitive and scientific spirit. In the early stages of the vaccine there were unforeseen problems; he suffered an adverse reaction, contracted a fever, and died on March 22, 1758.

One of the saddest elements of this episode is that, at the time of his death, Sarah had not yet moved to Princeton. Given the harsh winter and primitive forms of transportation, Jonathan made the journey to Princeton alone and planned for his wife to follow later in the spring.

Although separated from her by distance, Jonathan never lost the sense of Sarah's presence. In some of his last words, he spoke of the "uncommon union" that he and the young lady from New Haven had shared for thirty years. At his side were his daughters Lucy and Esther. Esther, who had lost her husband the previous year, now mourned the loss of her beloved father. The very next month Esther herself died from a similar reaction to the same smallpox vaccine. Not until that summer did Sarah arrive in Princeton. She contracted dysentery and died on October 2, 1758. She is buried next to her husband in the Princeton Cemetery.

Although he died at perhaps the prime of his writing and academic career and although he left behind many unfinished manuscripts and tasks (as he himself mentioned in his letter to Princeton's trustees), Edwards's accomplishments in his relatively short life were indeed a marvel. Yale University Press has embarked on publishing many of Edwards's works. The press plans to publish twenty-six volumes, but even these will contain only about half of his writings. Many other publishers, including the Banner of Truth, have also published various editions of Edwards's works, and all of his major treatises are readily available. He continues as a teacher of the church through these writings.

His legacy also lives on in his children, the ministerial candidates who apprenticed in his Northampton home, and the countless numbers influenced by his preaching. As he had resolved to do, Edwards lived with all of his might, and he did so to the glory of God.

A singular devotion to glorifying and enjoying God forever marks Edwards's life. As we have seen, this devotion worked itself out in a multitude of ways: in his "uncommon union" with Sarah and his love for his children; in his study and in his writing and preaching. Whether riding through the Connecticut River Valley or reading Paul's epistles, Edwards was awestruck by the beauty and harmony of God. He relished it. And he lived to point the way for others.

## Note on the Sources

Samuel Hopkins, Edwards's brother-in-law, provided the first account of Edwards's life. Sereno E. Dwight, Edwards's great-grandson, turned Hopkins's work into a narrative and produced the first real biography of Edwards. Dwight's biography is readily accessible in the Hickman edition of *The Works of Jonathan Edwards* (1834/1974), 1:xi–ccxxxiv. Other biographies of Edwards include Perry Miller's *Jonathan Edwards* (1949/1981) and Iain H. Murray's *Jonathan Edwards: A New Biography* (1987). The definitive source on the letters and other personal writings is George S. Claghorn's *Let-*

*ters and Personal Writings* (1998), volume 16 of the Yale edition of *The Works of Jonathan Edwards*. For the first time, all of the known letters written by Edwards are presented along with his *Resolutions,* diary, and "Personal Narrative." This volume also includes a helpful overview of Edwards's life and introductions to each individual letter and the various personal writings. (For full bibliographical information concerning the works mentioned here, see the Bibliography.)

# PART 2

## WRITINGS ON REVIVAL AND CHURCH LIFE

The selections discussed here span Edwards's ministry at Northampton. We begin with his first published sermon, "God Glorified in the Work of Redemption," given at the public lecture in Boston in 1731. Next follow three of his most famous and well-known treatises. In 1734–1735, revivals broke out in Northampton and neighboring towns. Edwards recorded the events and the stories of conversions in *A Faithful Narrative*. One decade later he published his fascinating study of true and genuine religion in *Treatise Concerning Religious Affections*. This section ends with his defense of his position on communion qualifications in *An Humble Inquiry*.

Together these texts constitute Edwards's central ideas and lasting contributions to the issues surrounding revival and church life. They are historical texts, born out of immediate circumstances. Yet, they transcend their eighteenth-century context and speak both to the church as a whole and to individual Christians today.

*3*

---

# ABSOLUTELY SOVEREIGN
## "God Glorified in the Work Of Redemption"

*The doctrine of God's sovereignty has very often
appeared an exceeding pleasant, bright, and sweet
doctrine to me: and absolute sovereignty is what I love to
ascribe to God.*

—Jonathan Edwards,
"Personal Narrative"

As he made the journey from Northampton to Boston during a hot July in 1731, Edwards's thoughts were no doubt fixed on the sermon he was about to preach. Speaking before the clergy and the elite of Boston on the Thursday lecture would be enough to unnerve even the most seasoned of pastors. But this was no ordinary public meeting. Being the first week of July, this particular Thursday lecture corresponded with the Harvard commencement. All of the alumni would be there, guaranteeing a packed house. Not only was this no ordinary meeting, but Edwards was not the typical speaker for such occasions.

The preface to the subsequently published version of his sermon reveals the strikes against Edwards even before he stepped into the pulpit. First, he was young. At twenty-eight

years of age, he fell far short of the years and accompany-
ing experience and wisdom of his auditors. As the preface
mentions, "It was with no small difficulty that the author's
youth and modesty were prevailed on to let him appear a
preacher in our public lecture." The preface additionally
notes the thankfulness of the Bostonian ministers that the
excellent ministry of the "venerable pastor" Solomon Stoddard appears to be in good hands in his grandson.

This accolade, however, came after he preached. Before
he preached, it was another story altogether. Stoddard had
earned the respect of these Bostonians, and the designation
of venerable pastor was no hollow compliment. Whether
young Jonathan would be able to stand in his grandfather's
shoes was probably in the back of his own mind and certainly in the minds of the audience. Finally, the preface
somewhat diminutively refers to "the college in the neighboring colony," an obvious reference to Yale. Edwards did
not share the Harvard credentials of the majority of his colleagues gathered in Boston for this occasion.

Being from Yale placed Edwards in a tenuous position.
Fearing the infiltration of latitudinarians at Harvard, certain ministers banded together to form Yale, this college in
Connecticut. Latitudinarianism simply means "tolerating
or allowing movement or latitude." In this case, the toler-
ance and latitude apply to adhering to the Westminster Confession of Faith and to orthodox Calvinism. Those concerned with this innovation at Harvard viewed this latitude
as the classic slippery slope that would eventually lead Harvard, and for that matter all of New England, into dire theological straits.

And so Yale began with an intense commitment to orthodox Calvinism. Sometime around 1720, however, which
was during Edwards's student days, the infamous "apostasy" occurred. Edwards stayed clear of this event, other

than to criticize it. Some of the tutors announced at graduation that they were leaving Congregationalism and becoming Anglicans. Not only had they moved in their church polity, but they had also renounced Calvinism, lining up with the latitudinarian camp of Anglicanism. Harvard might have Congregationalists not fully committed to Congregationalism and Calvinists not fully committed to Calvinism, but it sired no Anglicans and tolerated no Arminians. Where this particular Yale graduate stood theologically was something the Bostonians were anxious to know.

*look up/ study these*

## The Noble Doctrine

Edwards rose to the occasion, as evidenced in the publishing of the sermon. Thomas Prince and William Cooper, two Bostonian ministers, spoke for that audience of clergy when they wrote in the preface that "we quickly found [Edwards] a workman that needs not be ashamed [before] our brethren, our satisfaction was the greater when we saw him pitching upon so noble a subject, and treating it with so much strength and clearness, as the judicious reader will perceive in the following composure." The noble doctrine that Edwards pitched upon in the sermon is the central tenet of Calvinism and the central and all-encompassing theme of his life and writings.

It is the attribute that Edwards loved to ascribe to God: sovereignty. In typical Puritan fashion, Edwards states the doctrine of the sermon in a single sentence, exclaiming, "God is glorified in the work of redemption in this, that there appears in it so absolute and universal dependence of the redeemed on him."

Although Edwards came to love and to delight in this doctrine, such was not always the case. His "Personal Narrative" reveals that for some time Edwards stumbled over this doctrine as an obstacle to embracing God. Before he declares his sweet content with sovereignty, he writes, "From my childhood up, my mind had been wont to be full of objections against the doctrine of God's sovereignty, in choosing whom he would to eternal life, and rejecting whom he pleased." He then adds, "It used to appear like a horrible doctrine to me." But, somewhere along the way, Edwards's thoughts changed and he saw that God exercised his sovereignty according to justice and according to his pleasure.

Sovereignty is not akin to some abstract conception of fate, where the gods blindly, if not maliciously, manipulate human lives. Rather, the Triune God in his full complex of attributes decrees and acts in accordance with his Person. Having come to this conviction, Edwards writes, "There has been a wonderful alteration in my mind, with respect to the doctrine of God's sovereignty, from that day to this; so that I scarce ever have found so much as the rising of an objection against God's sovereignty in the most absolute sense, in showing mercy on whom he will show mercy, and hardening and eternally damning whom he will."

But, by Edwards's own account, while this was a conviction, he did not delight in it. That, too, however, changed. Again, Edwards remembers, "I have often since, not only had a conviction, but a delightful conviction." He then concludes, "The doctrine of God's sovereignty has very often appeared an exceeding pleasant, bright, and sweet doctrine to me: and absolute sovereignty is what I love to ascribe to God."

In this sermon we see Edwards not only carefully explaining this doctrine, but relishing it as well. It is clear from the application section of the sermon that Edwards intends his thoughts to show the flaws of Arminianism, and thus keep it in check. He does not accomplish this, however, by attacking it or by offering a stinging critique of its adherents. Instead, he presents the doctrine of sovereignty in all of its glory and luster, and in the process makes any alternative look entirely undesirable.

## The Anatomy of a Sermon

Like all Puritan sermons, this one contains three main sections, including the text, the doctrine, and the application. Edwards chose 1 Corinthians 1:29–31 as his text. Here Paul teaches that we have no grounds for boasting in ourselves: "It is because of him [God] that you are in Christ Jesus, who has become for us wisdom from God— that is, our righteousness, holiness and redemption. Therefore, as it is written: 'Let him who boasts boast in the Lord.' " (1 Cor. 1:30–31) He then offers a brief exposition of this text.

The bulk of the sermon explains the doctrine that derives from this text. Again following the Puritan tradition, Edwards offers a series of numbered points and subpoints clarifying, illustrating, and proving the doctrine. Finally, he offers the application, which the Puritans alternatively referred to as the "improvement" or, as he calls it here, the "use" section. Like the doctrine section, this part also contains numbered points as it lays out for the auditors the implications of the doctrine and the difference it should make in their lives. We will walk through each of these sections, unfolding Edwards's treatment of his delightful conviction.

Edwards begins his exposition of the text by drawing attention to the tendency of Greek culture to celebrate human wisdom and accomplishment. The gospel, despite its appearing to be foolish, destroys both as it confounds the wise and lays bare the strong. But this, Edwards notes, was God's plan all along. God so ordered his plan of redemption as to bring all of the glory to himself, and we are left with no cause to boast in ourselves.

God's aim in this work of redemption, Edwards observes, is ultimately "that man should not glory in himself, but in God alone." He then notes that God achieves this goal by making all humanity entirely dependent upon him "for all their good," and he proves his point by making three observations.

First, as the text reads, Christ "has become for us wisdom from God—that is, our righteousness, holiness, and redemption." So, Edwards writes, "All the good of the fallen and redeemed creature is concerned in these four things, and cannot be better distributed than into them; but Christ is each of them to us, and we have none of them otherwise than in him." Through Christ we have true knowledge and understanding; through Christ we have justification as our sins are pardoned and we have found favor with God; through Christ we have "true excellency of heart"; and through Christ we have "the actual deliverance from all misery and the bestowment of all happiness and glory."

Not only is Christ the source of all our good, but we do not earn Christ somehow by our merits; God graciously gives him to us. Further, Edwards's third observation notes that God graciously gives us the faith in Christ whereby we receive his blessings. These three observations reveal the absolute dependence of the redeemed upon God—that is, God the Father, Son, and Holy Spirit.

## Redemption and the Triune God

Paul ends his thought in this passage by quoting Jeremiah 9:24: "Let him who boasts boast in the Lord." Edwards takes this as a reference to the Triune Lord and proceeds to point out that redemption is a Trinitarian work that glorifies the Father, the Son, and the Holy Spirit. So Edwards concludes his exposition of the text by declaring our dependence on each member of the Trinity:

> We are dependent on Christ the Son of God, as he is our wisdom, righteousness, sanctification, and redemption. We are dependent on the Father, who has given us Christ, and made him to be these things to us. We are dependent on the Holy Spirit, for it is of him that we are in Christ Jesus; it is the Spirit of God that gives faith in him, whereby we receive him, and close with him.

Although this exposition of the text is brief, it nonetheless touches upon some weighty theological themes that engaged Edwards's mind throughout his life. Among these towers God's purpose in redemption, which also leads to his purpose for the world on a grand scale and his purpose for individuals on a personal scale. In fact, this theme will come to be one of Edwards's major sermon series eventually published in his *History of the Work of Redemption.*

God's purpose in redemption is also the subject of one of the last treatises that Edwards wrote, *Concerning the End for Which God Created the World.* In this present sermon we see only the tip of the iceberg as Edwards's mind begins turning over these ideas. Here he sees the work of the members of the Trinity in terms of God's decree, Christ's sacrifice, and the Spirit's application.

Just a few years earlier, Edwards drafted his "Essay on the Trinity." Again the seminal ideas in this essay reoccur again and again throughout his writings. Edwards was fascinated by the idea of the Trinity and the more he explored this central teaching of God in three Persons, the more he saw of the wonder of God and the more he stood in awe of the Creator, Redeemer, and Sanctifier. And the more his writings unfolded the contours of this complex and awe-inspiring doctrine.

## Absolute and Universal Dependence

On this particular day, however, Edwards focused on the sovereignty of God. He declares the doctrine derived from this text as the following: "God is glorified in the work of redemption in this, that there appears in it so absolute and universal a dependence of the redeemed on him." He makes two points about our dependence, noting its absolute and universal nature. He first develops each of these, and then shows how our *absolute* and *universal* dependence does in fact bring glory to God. By *absolute* he means the whole or entire individual, and by *universal* he intends all of humanity.

To show that in fact all of humanity is entirely dependent upon God, he cleverly employs three propositions. Edwards argues that as the redeemed we have all our good *of, through,* and *in* God (see fig. 3.1)

Each of these deserves unpacking in order to get at these important insights. First, Edwards observes that not only is God the author and first cause of our good, "but he is the *only* proper cause." God gives Christ as Redeemer, and he also gives the faith that we have in Christ. Further, God has given not only the Son, but also the Spirit, the means of grace, Scripture, and even the ministers who faithfully proclaim the gospel. God does all of this as a wonderful demonstration of his grace. Edwards observes that the grace of God is proportionate to both the gift and the benefit of the grace. The gift, of course, is God's own Son, God himself, and is of infinite value. So, too, is the benefit, as

---

**FIG. 3.1**

**Our Good**

| All of our good is | God is |
|---|---|
| *of* God | the source, cause, and author of our good |
| *through* God | the means and mediator of our good |
| *in* God | the end, object, and essence of our good |

---

we are delivered from an infinite and eternal misery to infinite and eternal joy and glory.

The magnitude of God's grace also enjoys a proportionate relationship to the great unworthiness of its recipients. Because of our participation in Adam's fall, we stand in dire need of God's grace and are utterly unable to merit it in any way on our own. Edwards paints the reality of our fallen state as a condition of sin, misery, helplessness, and insufficiency. We stand before God "naked and wholly without any good." Yet, through God's grace, we are abundantly "enriched with all good." Not only does God as the author of redemption display his grace, but this grace also shines forth his power. God's power converts, preserves, and will someday perfect his redeemed. Redemption is one grand and "wonderful exercise of his power."

Second, our good comes *through* God as the Triune God authored our salvation and also mediates our redemption. And, Edwards observes, we have an absolute dependence on this mediation. Here Edwards makes the point that God not only provides the mediator, he is the mediator. He notes that God purchased our redemption, then adds, "Yea God is both the purchaser and the price; for Christ, who is God, purchased these blessings for us, by offering up himself as the price of our salvation." Consequently, it is Christ's righteousness that is applied to our account, canceling out our debt of sin. It is because of or *through* Christ that we stand before God.

In his third point, Edwards eloquently expresses the idea that all that is good, excellent, and beautiful is *in* God. Thus not only does he originate and mediate all our good, but he himself is our good. He is our joy, delight, and pleasure. This extraordinary concept was a personal breakthrough in Edwards's own thinking about God, and the emphasis he places on it in his works constitutes one of his great gifts to the church.

Here he discusses God as our good by designating two different types, the objective good and the inherent good. God is the objective good in the sense that he is the object of our good. Edwards explains: "God himself is the great good which [the redeemed] are brought to the possession and enjoyment of by redemption. He is the highest good, and the sum of all that good which Christ purchased. God is the inheritance of the saints; he is the portion of their souls." He continues: "God is their wealth and treasure, their food, their life, their dwelling place, their ornament and diadem, and their everlasting honor and glory." To be sure, Edwards notes that we enjoy other things, and also enjoy each other, for that matter. But nothing compares to that delight we have in God.

Edwards illustrates his intention behind the designation of inherent good by drawing an analogy of the sun and planets to God and the redeemed. He explains, "The saints are beautiful and blessed by a communication of God's holiness and joy, as the moon and planets are bright by the sun's light." The saints "have spiritual excellency and joy by a kind of participation of God." What he means here is that we have spiritual excellency in ourselves, not, of course, because of anything we have done, but only through our union with Christ. Edwards is stressing here the communion and fellowship that we have with God as we are invited into the glorious fellowship of the Trinity.

This leads Edwards to examine the unique function of the Holy Spirit as indwelling the saints and enabling this deep communion. So Edwards declares, "It is by partaking of the Holy Spirit, that [the saints] have communion with Christ in his fullness." Edwards bases his thoughts here on John 7:38–39. In verse 38, Christ exclaims, "Whoever believes in me, as the Scripture has said, streams of living water will flow from within him." John then adds the editorial in verse 39, "By this he meant the Spirit, whom those who believed in him were later to receive." "Herein," Edwards notes, "consists the fullness of good."

Edwards also finds this teaching in the intriguing synoptic parallel of Matthew 7:11 and Luke 11:13. The two texts are strikingly similar, yet with one significant difference. Matthew 7:11 reads, "If you, then, though you are evil, know how to give good gifts to your children, how much more will your Father in heaven give good gifts to those who ask him!" Luke 11:13 reads, "If you then, though you are evil, know how to give good gifts to your children, how much more will your Father in heaven give the Holy Spirit to those who ask him!" Edwards combines the two texts and concludes that the good gift is the Holy Spirit. And, life in the Spirit is life in communion and fellowship with the Triune God. Indeed, God *is* our good.

## The Luster of God's Glory

Edwards's next point argues that because of our absolute and universal dependence, God is in fact glorified. He then offers some further reasons to support his claim. The first is a rather simple concept, but one that can often be overlooked. Edwards writes, "Dependence does especially tend to command and oblige the attention and observation." In other words, because we are dependent, we notice God. Like infants dependent upon the care of a parent, humanity draws even its breath by the mercy and care of God. In masquerading as self-sufficient, however, humanity vainly attempts to assert its independence.

Sadly, this mind-set runs deep in our culture. A rather popular television show once contained a scene in which the child star was asked to pray for a meal. The prayer went like this: "Dear God, we paid for this ourselves, so thanks for nothing." The reality of the situation is quite the reverse. Redemption reveals our true nature as we see our helplessness and utter insufficiency. Because of the great level of our dependence, God and "his glory are the more directly set in our view." And, a sincere and grateful "thanks for everything" is the only proper response. As Edwards concludes, "How unreasonable and ungrateful we should be, if we did not acknowledge that sufficiency and glory which we absolutely, immediately, and universally depend upon!"

This sense of independence endemic to human nature leads to the inverse perspective of a high view of humanity and a low view of God. As Edwards notes, "So much the more men exalt themselves, so much the less they will surely be disposed to exalt God." But, and this is his second reason proving that redemption glorifies God, if we realize the dependence that we have on God, then we see that "God is infinitely above everything." In the work of redemption we see that "God should appear full, and man in himself empty, that God should appear all, and humanity nothing." Redemption restores both God and humanity to their proper place and causes the latter to ascribe to God the glory and honor due him.

Edwards's third reason essentially summarizes all that he has said so far and leads into the application section of the sermon. He reiterates the notion that our dependence upon God is not partial, but total and complete, so that, again, nothing detracts from the glory of God. He then presents four implications of this doctrine. The first point essentially summarizes the doctrine section. Reading between the lines, however, Edwards calls upon his audience to marvel at the work of redemption, never to lose the wonder of admiring God's work, and to acknowledge the dependence that we have on God.

Second (and here enters his critique of Arminianism, though he does not call it by name), Edwards notes that "those doctrines and schemes of divinity that are in any respect opposite to such an absolute and universal dependence on God, derogate from his glory, and thwart the design of our redemption." He adds, "Whatever scheme is inconsistent with our *entire* dependence on God for all, and of having all of him, through him, and in him, is repugnant to the design and tenor of the gospel and robs it of that which God accounts its lustre and glory."

The doctrine of sovereignty does not lend itself to being a convenient doctrine. That is, God is not sovereign when it suits us or just when we allow him, and he is not sovereign partially. He is sovereign universally and absolutely. Edwards's third point concerns faith. It makes perfect sense, Edwards argues, that faith serves as the means by which we come into redemption as it causes us to realize our inability and our dependence upon God. As Edwards writes, "Faith abases men, and exalts God, it gives all the glory of redemption to him alone." Further, faith reflects the proper attitude of humility, "the great ingredient of true faith."

In humility, we come to Christ and so we join in Edwards's affirmation of the Psalmist, declaring, "Not to us,

O LORD, not to us but to your name be the glory" (Ps. 115:1). This leads to Edwards's fourth and final point, which I have reproduced here in full:

> Let us be exhorted to exalt God alone, and ascribe to him all the glory of redemption. Let us endeavor to obtain, and increase in, a sensibleness of our great dependence, to have our eye on him alone, to mortify a self-dependent and self-righteous disposition. Man is naturally exceeding prone to exalt himself, and depend on his own power of goodness; as though from himself he must expect happiness. He is prone to have respect to enjoyments alien from God and his Spirit, as those in which happiness is to be found. But this doctrine should teach us to exalt God *alone*: as by trust and reliance, so by praise. *Let him that glorieth, glory in the Lord.* Hath any man hope that he is converted, and sanctified, and that his mind is endowed with that true excellency and spiritual beauty? That his sins are forgiven, and he received into God's favor, and exalted to the honor and blessedness of being his child, and an heir of eternal life? Let him give God all the glory; who alone makes him to differ from the worst of men in this world, or the most miserable of the damned in hell. Hath any man much comfort and strong hope of eternal life, let not his hope lift him up, but to dispose him the more to abase himself, to reflect on his own exceeding unworthiness of such a favor, and to exalt God alone. Is any man eminent in holiness, and abundant in good works, let him take nothing of the glory of it to himself, but ascribe it to him whose 'workmanship we are, created in Christ Jesus unto good works.'

The preface to the first published edition of this sermon insightfully observes the implication of the doctrine of sovereignty. Thomas Prince and William Cooper observe, "For in proportion to the sense we have of our dependence on the sovereign God for all the good we want, will be our value for him, our application to him, our trust in him, our fear to offend him, and our care to please him." The preface also points to the danger of neglecting or softening this doctrine as the authors add, "We hope [these doctrines] will never grow unfashionable among us: for we are well assured, if those which call the doctrines of grace ever come to be contemned or disrelished, vital piety will proportionately languish and wear away."

Edwards himself viewed his relationship to the doctrine of sovereignty as pivotal to his understanding of and relationship to God. For Edwards, matters of theology and issues of the Christian life were not in conflict, but in perfect concert. Christian living, Edwards argued, issues from good theology, and no doctrine was more fundamental than the sovereignty of God in this work of redemption. Preaching on the doctrines of grace and displaying God's sovereignty consisted of much more than the Thursday Boston public lecture. It consistently marked Edwards's preaching, and over the course of a few years, he witnessed the results in his congregation at Northampton.

## Note on the Sources

The sermon "God Glorified in the Work of Redemption" is available in the Hickman edition of *The Works of Jonathan Edwards* (1834/1974), 2:2–7. It may also be found in *The Sermons of Jonathan Edwards: A Reader* (1999), pages 66–82. The "Personal Narrative" is in George S. Claghorn's *Letters and Personal Writings* (1998), volume 16 of the Yale edition of *The Works of Jonathan Edwards,* pages 790–804; and in *A Jonathan Edwards Reader* (1995), pages 281–96. Parts of the "Personal Narrative" appear throughout Sereno E. Dwight's "Memoir of Jonathan Edwards" in the Hickman edition of *The Works of Jonathan Edwards* (1834/1974), 1:xi–ccxxxiv.

*4*

# THE SURPRISING WORK OF GOD

## *A Faithful Narrative*

*Thus sometimes when persons have seemed evidently to
be stripped of all their own righteousness, and to have
stood self-condemned as guilty of death, they have been
comforted with a joyful and satisfying view, that the
mercy and grace of God is sufficient for them.*
—Jonathan Edwards,
*A Faithful Narrative*

The publishing of Edwards's first book was not by his
own design. In May 1735, he wrote a letter to
Bostonian minister Benjamin Colman relaying the
stories of the revivals in Northampton and other towns in
the Connecticut River Valley. Colman sent a large portion
of the letter to his friend and fellow pastor in London, John
Guyse, who in turn shared it with both his congregation and
the famous hymn writer Isaac Watts. Guyse's congregation,
Watts, and Colman all wanted to hear more. Colman
quickly sent off a letter to Edwards requesting that he expand the letter so that it might be published. Colman first
published the letter along with two sermons of Edwards's
uncle William Williams in Boston in 1736.

Not content with the letter, Watts and Guyse wanted the whole story and asked for still more from the pen of Edwards. Once again Edwards set out to expand his account and eventually sent a full manuscript to them. Guyse and Watts then shepherded the manuscript through the press and in London in 1737 *A Faithful Narrative of the Surprizing Work of God in the Conversion of Many Hundred Souls in Northampton, and the Neighboring Towns and Villages of New-Hampshire in New-England* was published.

It was not, however, the colony of *New* Hampshire. It was Hampshire County. But this was not the only thing that Watts and Guyse were to get wrong. A copy of their edition eventually made it back across the Atlantic and into the hands of its author. In the flyleaf of his copy, which is now in the Beineke rare book collection at Yale University, Edwards wrote:

> It must be noted that the Rev. publishers of the ensuing narrative, by much abridging of it, and altering the phrase and manner of expression, and not strictly observing the words of the original, have through mistake, published some things diverse from fact, which is the reason that some words are crossed out: and besides there are some mistakes in the preface, which are noted in the margin.

He started on the title page crossing out the word *New* and continued from there. In 1738 Edwards guided his own edition through the Boston press and *A Faithful Narrative* emerged again, only this time strictly observing his words and faithful to his intent.

Edwards probably did not anticipate his letter to Colman becoming his first book (and he certainly did not expect to encounter such problems in getting a book published!). But then, the revivals themselves, as the full title announces, also

*8.7.23.*

*A Faithful*

# NARRATIVE

OF THE

## Surprizing Work of GOD

IN THE

# CONVERSION

OF

Many HUNDRED SOULS in *Northampton*, and the Neighbouring Towns and Villages of ~~New~~-Hampfhire in *New-England*.

In a LETTER to the Rev^d. Dr. BENJAMIN COLMAN of *Bofton*.

Written by the Rev^d. Mr. EDWARDS, Minifter of *Northampton*, on *Nov*. 6. 1736.

And Publifhed,

## With a Large PREFACE,

By Dr. WATTS and Dr. GUYSE.

*L O N D O N*;

Printed for JOHN OSWALD, at the *Rofe and Crown*, in the *Poultry*, near *Stocks-Market*. M.DCC.XXXVII.

Price flitch'd 1*s*. Bound in Calf-Leather, 1*s*. 6*d*.

Title page from Edwards's personal copy of the Watts and Guyse edition of *A Faithful Narrative*. Edwards crossed out the word *New*, as Watts and Guyse mistakenly took the Connecticut county of Hampshire for the colony of New Hampshire.

came as a surprise. A few years had passed since Edwards delivered his Boston lecture, "God Glorified in the Work of Redemption." From his pulpit he continued to herald the sovereignty of God in salvation and did not grow tired of preaching the doctrines of grace. In those few years evidence that lives were affected by such preaching began to surface in his congregation and in the congregations of his fellow Connecticut River Valley ministers.

## Northampton Harvests

It all started among the young people of the church. As Edwards observes, "At the latter end of the year 1733, there appeared a very unusual flexibleness, and yielding to advice, in our young people." When we think of colonial times, we typically do so rather nostalgically and naively. Edwards's comments here remind us that certain tendencies toward rebellion and stubbornness are indeed endemic to human nature and span the generations. He extols the virtues of a sudden openness to, in Puritan terminology, religious instruction, or as we may say, the things of God.

Revival was nothing new to the members of the Northampton congregation. Edwards begins his *Faithful Narrative* with an abbreviated history of the town and the church, drawing attention to the five "harvests" or seasons of revivals under the ministry of his grandfather and predecessor, Solomon Stoddard. But the last one was eighteen years ago, and a cloud of indifference had settled over the town in matters pertaining to religion.

What accounted for this newfound openness? In his narrative, Edwards attributes it to two things. First, as it does in our lives today, tragedy and the sudden loss of life can shake us from complacency, and it did just that in the 1730s. A few younger people in neighboring towns died suddenly, leaving behind stirring testimonies that "seemed much to contribute to the solemnizing of the spirits of many young persons: and there evidently to appear more of a religious concern on people's minds."

Second, there was a most unexpected work of God in converting a particular person in Edwards's own town of Northampton. He discreetly refers to her as a "company keeper," which more than likely meant that she was a prostitute. When she came to meet with Edwards, he didn't think she was "in any wise serious." He soon changed his mind as she relayed her story of her own conversion and testified to the work of God in her life. Edwards concluded "that what she gave an account of was a glorious work of God's infinite power and sovereign grace; and that God had given her a new heart, truly broken and sanctified."

He, however, feared that the congregation would not rejoice with her but instead look upon her with contempt. Again he was surprised: "The event was the reverse, to a wonderful degree; God made it, I suppose, the greatest occasion of awakening to others, of anything that ever came to pass in the town." Edwards makes a rather self-effacing comment, attributing the revivals not to his own preaching so much as to this unlikely instrument used by God. In his view, the display of grace in this anonymous woman's life sparked the revival.

He summarizes the immediate effect of her conversion when he writes, "Presently upon this, a great and earnest concern about the great things of religion and the eternal world became universal in all parts of the town, and among persons of all degrees and all ages; the noise amongst the dry bones waxed louder and louder." When Edwards mentions people of all ages, he means it. As his narrative continues, he devotes a great number of pages to the story of

Phebe Bartlet, a true heroine of colonial literature and religious history at a remarkable four years of age.

Before he gets to Phebe's story, however, Edwards discusses the revivals in general and uses the occasion to offer his rather insightful comments and observations on conversion and the surprising work of God. He describes every pastor's and every congregation's dream when he writes the following description of life in Northampton during the height of the revival:

> This work of God, as it was carried on, and the number of true saints multiplied, soon made a glorious alteration in the town; so that in the spring and summer following, *anno* 1735, the town seemed to be full of the presence of God: it never was so full of love, nor so full of joy; and yet so full of distress, as it was then. There were remarkable tokens of God's presence in almost every house. It was a time of joy in families on the account of salvation's being brought unto them; parents rejoicing over their children as newborn, and husbands over their wives, and wives over their husbands. The goings on of God were seen in his sanctuary (Psalm 68:24), God's day was a delight, and his tabernacles were amiable (Psalm 84:1). Our public assemblies were then beautiful; the congregation was alive in God's service, everyone earnestly intent on the public worship, every hearer eager to drink in the words of the minister as they came from his mouth; the assembly in general were, from time to time in tears while the Word was preached; some weeping with sorrow and distress, others with joy and love, others with pity and concern for the souls of their neighbors.

Many elements of this selection deserve comment. Notice that Edwards looks for and then finds the results of the revival in the lives that it changes. He sees this divine work of transforming lives as starting in the home and cultivating harmonious relationships as loved ones are brought together in Christ. From the home it spreads to the church and brings with it a desire to worship and to hear the Word preached. And then it moves even further as it expresses itself in love and concern for one's neighbor.

This scenario repeated itself in towns throughout the Connecticut River Valley. It even foreshadows the Great Awakening as Edwards refers to revivals among "some peoples of the Jerseys," mentioning William and Gilbert Tennent, the sons of William Tennent Sr., the founder of Log College, which eventually became Princeton University. Returning to Northampton, Edwards estimates that "more than 300 souls were savingly brought home to Christ in this town in the space of half a year." The church grew so much that it immediately embarked upon a major building project, enlarging the meetinghouse.

### Edwards's Theology of Revival

It was a wonderful time, "full of the presence of God." Edwards notes, however, that this time of Awakening was also a time "full of distress," a time when tears of sorrow equally matched tears of joy. This distress was due to nothing other than an impassioned sense of sin and its consequences. As a jeweler displays the radiance of a diamond against a dark cloth, so Edwards allowed the radiance of Christ and his mercy to shine forth against the doleful corruption of the sin that reigns in the human soul. This conviction of sinfulness brings us, in Edwards's words, "off from all self-confidence" and leads us to "absolute dependence on [God's] sovereign power and grace." It further leads us to Christ, our indispensable mediator, without whom no one can stand before God.

Sin brings us face to face with our inability, and we have nothing left to do but to throw ourselves to "the infinite mercy of God and all-sufficiency of Christ." This is the first step that we take as we come to Christ in humiliation, standing with empty hands and guilty hearts and then discovering "the mercy of God through Christ." Edwards here touches upon the rather old-fashioned notion of human inability and utter sinfulness—the same theme that permeates his Boston lecture four years earlier.

His revival preaching did see tears of joy and hearts full of praise, but it also witnessed the harsh realities of sin and its consequences. He spoke plainly and straightforwardly of the plight of humanity, noting that because of our dreadful corruption, pride, unbelief, and stubborn and obstinate wills, God is "wholly just and righteous in rejecting [us], and all that [we] do, and casting [us] off forever." This emphasis on sin sets Edwards apart from those who in later centuries would tout a gospel to so-called good-hearted people who just want to be a little better, a gospel that finds humanity not hopeless and helpless, but essentially good. Sin does not harmonize with the message of prosperity in such preaching, and all too often it gets jettisoned rather quickly. The reality of the matter is, however, that such a gospel is no gospel at all. Edwards knew that preaching on sin, as unpopular as it may be, is essential to faithfully preaching the gospel.

He also distances himself from other revivalists in his own day, as well as those who come on the scene later in the nineteenth century, through his emphasis not so much on the decision, which leads to counting converts as so many trophies, but rather on the changed life that follows. For Edwards, conversion results in evidence, in the fruit of the new life. He brings his ideas on this subject to full and clear expression in *Religious Affections* (1746), and we will explore his thought on these issues in the following chapter. Edwards here remarks upon humility as the tell-tale sign of a genuine convert:

> Such persons amongst us have been thus distinguished with the most extraordinary discoveries of God, have commonly in no wise appeared with the assuming, and self-conceited, and self-sufficient airs of enthusiasts; but exceedingly the contrary; and are eminent for a spirit of meekness, modesty, self-diffidence, and low opinion of themselves: no persons seem to be so sensible of their need of instruction, and so eager to receive it, as some of them, nor so ready to think others better than themselves. Those that have been thought to be converted amongst us have generally manifested a longing to lie low, and in the dust before God; withal complaining of their not being able to lie low enough.

Further, Edwards was not naïve. He fully realized that just because someone had some type of an experience, it didn't necessarily mean that the experience was genuine. And he knew that a profession of Christ was no certain guarantee of genuine conversion. Again, he explores this idea in *Religious Affections,* where he especially reflects a sensitivity not only to one's ability to deceive others, but also to the reality of self-deception. Here in *A Faithful Narrative,* he expresses his awareness of such potential deception:

> I am very sensible how apt many would be, if they should see the account I have here given, presently to think with themselves that I am very fond of making a great many converts, and of magnifying and aggrandizing the matter; and to think that, for want of judgment, I take every religious pang and enthusiastic conceit for saving conversion.

Edwards did not lack such judgment. In fact, he goes to great lengths to defend the events at Northampton as not an invention of his own making, but rather as a genuine work of God. To do so, he thought it best to discuss the nature of a true conversion, and so he embarks on such a description in the middle of the narrative.

## A Very Mysterious Thing

According to Edwards, the only two sure things about conversion are that it is "very various" and "very mysterious." By saying that conversion varies, he repudiates any attempts to make one's salvation automatic or formulaic. While there are certain elements that comprise salvation, such as the conviction of sin and faith in Christ, Edwards recognized that people are individuals who respond differently and display different effects.

People respond differently, for instance, to conviction of sin. Some, as Edwards notes, take such a conviction as a call to self-improvement and go through a series of failed attempts at self-reform and live rather frustrated lives. Their efforts only serve to obscure the grace of God, or as he puts it, "They set themselves upon a new course of fruitless endeavors in their own strengths to make themselves better." Such efforts, however, only bring about "new disappointments." He then continues:

> They don't know but there is something else to be done, in order to their obtaining converting grace, that they have never done yet. . . . Thus they wander about from mountain to hill, seeking rest and finding none: when they are beat out of one refuge they fly to another, till they are as it were debilitated, broken, and subdued with legal humblings; in which God gives them a conviction of their own utter helplessness and insufficiency, and discovers the true remedy.

Others, such as Phebe Bartlet, immediately come to see their own helplessness and take refuge in Christ in short order. Not only does conviction of sin vary, but one's response to Christ varies as well. So Edwards writes:

> Conversion is a great and glorious work of God's power, at once changing the heart and infusing life into the dead soul; though that grace then implanted does more gradually display itself in some than in others. But as to fixing on the precise time when they put forth the very first act of grace, there is a great deal of difference in different persons; in some it seems very discernible when the very time of this was; but others are more at a loss. In this respect, there are very many who don't know the time (as has been already observed), that when they have the first exercises of grace.

Today, in many circles, quite an emphasis gets placed on the decision one makes to come to Christ, and it is absolutely essential, according to some, that you know the precise time, place, and circumstances. I have known some who agonize over whether or not they are converted because they can't remember a specific time and place. Edwards disagrees with such a view, and he offers comforting assurance to those who express such doubts. Some may come to Christ rather suddenly, in the midst of a crisis or some cataclysmic event in their lives. For others this may not be the case, but it would be wrong, in Edwards's view, to force everybody into the same mold. He wants us to see that God works in different people in different ways. He concludes his point with the following observation:

> There is an endless variety in the particular manner and circumstances in which persons are wrought on, and an opportunity of seeing so much of such a work of God will show that God is further from confining himself to certain steps,

and a particular method, in his work on souls, than it may be some do imagine. I believe it has occasioned some good people amongst us, that were before too ready to make their own experiences a rule to others, to be less censorious and more extended in their charity. The work of God has been glorious in its variety, it has the more displayed the manifoldness and unsearchableness of the wisdom of God, and wrought more charity amongst its people.

Consequently, he remarks that "the manner of God's work on the soul is sometimes especially very mysterious." While there may be variety to God's work in salvation, and while there is mystery involved as well, one thing that you can count on is that a genuine work of God in conversion results in two elements. The first involves a certain conviction of the truth of the gospel. In other words, one who stands redeemed may have assurance of salvation. The second element that flows from conversion is a changed life.

Concerning the first element, Edwards points out that "the converting influences of God's Spirit very commonly bring an extraordinary conviction of the reality and certainty of the great things of religion (though in some this is much

---

**FIG. 4.2**

**Major Writings on Revival**

1737  *A Faithful Narrative of the Surprizing Work of God*

1741  *The Distinguishing Marks of a Work of the Spirit of God*

1742  *Some Thoughts Concerning the Present Revival of Religion in New-England*

1746  *A Treatise Concerning Religious Affections*

---

greater, some time after conversion, than at first); they have that sight and taste of the divinity, or divine excellency, that there is in the things of the gospel, that is more to convince them than reading many volumes of arguments without it." They come to be "convinced of the truth of the gospel in general, and that the Scriptures are the Word of God." Edwards will spend a great deal of time dealing with conviction and certainty in his treatise on *Religious Affections,* and we will return to this idea in the following chapter.

Conversion brings with it not only a certain conviction, but also a changed life. In short, everything, Edwards observes, is new. Just like his own experience recorded in his "Personal Narrative," it is as if the new Christian sees everything for the first time. Here, Edwards expresses it this way: "Persons after their conversion often speak of things of religion as seeming new to them; that preaching is a new thing . . . that the Bible is a new book: they find there new chapters, new psalms, new histories, because they see them in a new light."

Conversion also sinks its roots deep into the soul and brings forth a whole new life that not only sees differently but also thinks and acts differently. Edwards writes that new converts had a great and wonderful delight in both Scripture and the Lord's Day and that "our converts then remarkably appeared united in dear affection to one another, and many have expressed much of that spirit of love which they felt toward all mankind; and particularly to those that had been least friendly to them."

He then shows that this love demonstrated itself in action: "Never, I believe, was so much done in confessing injuries, and making up differences as the last year." He adds, "Persons after their own conversion have commonly expressed an exceeding desire for the conversion of others: some have thought they should be willing to die for the conversion of any soul, though of one of the meanest of their fellow creatures and one of their worst enemies; and many have indeed been in great distress with desires and longings for it."

## Phebe Bartlet

Until now, Edwards's discussion of conversion in the narrative has consisted of general and abstract statements. He concludes the narrative by making his generalizations concrete by relating the accounts of two people: Abigail Hutchinson and Phebe Bartlet. Edwards relates their stories in order "to give a clearer idea of the nature and manner of the operation of God's Spirit, in this wonderful effusion of it." Below follow lengthy excerpts from the story of Phebe Bartlet.

Edwards's choice of a young girl as a model of a genuine conversion and the devout life that follows was rather enlightened for the time. But young Phebe was a wise choice, as her life provides one of the most remarkable stories of the colonial revivals and of the surprising work of God. Edwards relates the following account:

> She was born in March, in the year 1731. About the latter end of April, or beginning of May, 1735, she was greatly affected by the talk of her brother, who had been hopefully converted a little before, at about eleven years of age, and then seriously talked to her about the great things of religion. Her parents did not know it at that time and were not wont, in the councils they gave to their children, particularly to direct themselves to her, by reason of her being so young, and as they supposed not capable of understanding: but after her brother had talked to her, they observed her very earnestly listen to the advice they gave to the other children; and she was observed very constantly to retire several times in a day, as was concluded, for secret prayer. . . .

On Thursday, the last day of July, about the middle of the day, the child being in the closet where she used to retire, her mother heard her speaking aloud; which was unusual and never heard of before. And her voice seemed to be as one of exceeding importunate and engaged; but her mother could distinctly hear only these words (spoken in her childish manner, but seemed to be spoken with extraordinary earnestness, and out of distress of soul): "Pray, blessed Lord, give me salvation! I pray, beg, pardon all of my sins!" When the child had done prayer, she came out of the closet, and came and sat down by her mother, and cried out loud . . . she continued thus earnestly crying, and taking on for some time, till at length she suddenly ceased crying and began to smile, and presently said with a smiling countenance, "Mother the kingdom of heaven is come to me!"

Her mother was surprised at the sudden alteration, and at the speech; and knew not what to make of it, but at first said nothing to her. The child presently spoke again, and said, "There is another come to me, and there is another; there is three." And being asked what she meant, she answered, "One is Thy will be done; and there is another Enjoy him forever"; by which it seems that when the child said, "There is three come to me," she meant three passages of the catechism that came to her mind.

After the child had said this, she retired again into her closet; and her mother went over to her brother's, who was next neighbor; and when she came back, the child, being come out of the closet, meets her mother with this cheerful speech, "I can find God now!" referring to what she had before complained of that she could not find God. Then the child spoke again, and said, "I love God!" Her mother asked her how well she loved God, whether she loved God better than her father and mother; she said, "Yes." Then she asked her whether she loved better than her little sister Rachel. She answered, "Yes, better than anything!"

Then her elder sister referring to her saying that she could find God now, asked her where she could find God. She answered, "In heaven." "Why," said she, "have you been in heaven?" "No," said the child. By this it seems not to have been any imagination of anything seen with bodily eyes, that she called God, when she said, "I can find God now." Her mother asked whether she was afraid of going to hell, and that made her cry. She answered, "Yes, I was; but now I shan't." Her mother asked whether she thought that God had given her salvation. She answered, "Yes." Her mother asked her, when. She answered, "Today."

That evening as she lay abed, she called one of her little cousins to her that was present in the room, as having something to say to him; and when he came, she told him that heaven was better than earth. The next day being Friday, her mother asking her her catechism, asked her what God made her for. She answered, "To serve him," and added, "everybody should serve God, and get an interest in Christ."

Phebe's newfound joy is matched by her zeal to proclaim Christ and to begin to live for him. In fact, Edwards continues to relay how Christ had changed young Phebe's life. He mentions that "she seems to love God's house, and is very eager to go there." Her mother asked her if it was only to see all of the fine people. Phebe answered that she went "to hear Edwards preach." Edwards further relays one particular story that demonstrates her sensitivity and her awareness of sin and its impact on her life. He notes that she has "very much the fear of God before her eyes (Ps. 36:1), and an extraordinary dread of sin against him." This is clear in the following account:

Some time in August, the last year, she went with some bigger children to get some plums in a neighbor's lot, knowing nothing of any harm for what she did; but when she brought some of the plums into the house, her mother mildly reproved her and told her that she must not get plums without permission, because it was sin: God had commanded her not to steal. The child seemed greatly surprised, and burst out into tears, and cried out, "I won't have these plums!" and turning to her sister Eunice, very earnestly said to her, "Why did you ask me to go to that plum tree? I should not have gone if you had not asked me."

The other children did not seem to be much affected or concerned; but there was no pacifying Phebe. Her mother told [her] she might go and ask permission, and then it would not be sin for [her] to eat them; and sent one of the children to that end; and when she returned, her mother had told her that the owner had given permission, now she might eat them, and it would not be stealing. This stilled her a little while; but presently she broke out again into an exceeding fit of crying: her mother asked her what made her cry again; why she cried now, since they had asked permission. What it was that troubled her now? And asked her several times very earnestly, before she made any answer; but at last she said it was because—*because it was sin!*

She continued a considerable time crying; and said that she would not go again if Eunice had asked her an hundred times; and she retained her aversion to that fruit for a considerable time, under the remembrance of her former sin.

What may have been for others a routine action that came with little consequence was for Phebe a rather serious offense that greatly affected her. Phebe's young, sensitive spirit speaks volumes to our more mature abilities to rationalize our actions and to condone our sins. We also see her resolve not to sin as she would say no a hundred times over to an opportunity to pick those plums again. And we see her aversion to sin and its dreaded consequences rather vividly in "her aversion to that fruit for a considerable time."

## Reflections on Revival

*A Faithful Narrative* tells the story of the revivals at Northampton in the mid-1730s. It also offers great insight into the nature of conversion and the changed life that follows, themes that come to dominate a full decade of Edwards's thought and writings. By the end of 1736, when Edwards pens his narrative, the revival had ebbed and receded and Edwards lamented its loss. In just a few short years, however, Edwards would once again find himself in the midst of another surprising work of God in the Great Awakening. Edwards continued his faithful preaching of the doctrines of grace, explaining again and again the sinfulness and helplessness of humanity and the infinite grace and mercy of Christ. Although more will be said about the Great Awakening and its impact on Edwards and on the colonial church in the following chapter, a few words concerning the whole context of Edwards's thought on revival and revivalism are in order.

Edwards is usually interpreted as standing in a long line of human instruments used by God to bring revival to a dead and decaying church. He also stands at the beginning of the line of revivals in this country, although as pointed out above, as well as by others, he differs extensively from many of his successors. While it is certainly right to think of Edwards as a revivalist, there are some elements to the thought of Edwards on the revivals and revivalism that are not so well known, but are truly informative and perhaps beneficial for the church.

Many years after both the revivals in 1735 and the Great Awakening, in 1750 Edwards wrote a letter to his Scottish friend Thomas Gillespie. He writes, "Doubtless at that time there was a very glorious work of God wrought in Northampton, and there were numerous instances of saving conversion; though undoubtedly many were deceived, and deceived others; and the number of true converts was not so great as was then imagined." Despite his own efforts to safeguard his estimation of the revival, even Edwards himself admitted that the picture was not all that it had appeared to be.

The numbers, however, are not the point. Edwards expresses something deeper in his concern with the revivals and their effects. What Edwards fully learned from these experiences is that time matters. In this lengthy letter to Gillespie, Edwards rehearses for his transatlantic correspondent the problems that eventually led to his dismissal from Northampton, which we will pick up in chapter 6. The thrust of the letter, however, offers a great deal of insight into Edwards's mature philosophy of ministry. Edwards remarks that the healthy church, while experiencing seasons of revival, *consistently* bears fruit. So it is with the individual Christian life.

Revivalists, and those seeking revival, look for the quick fix, the immediate result, genuine or not as the case may be. Edwards learned that it's the long haul that matters. The experience of true religion is week in and week out. It is in the daily task and in the ordinary, rather than simply a passing fad that loses its appeal as soon as the excitement wears thin. In 1736, Edwards wondered what happened to those who expressed such zeal just one year earlier. In 1746, he questioned the sincerity of the experiences of the early 1740s when the once full pews regularly looked sparse, and by 1750, still sure that God did a "great and glorious work," he puzzled over the lack of long-term and consistent commitment of both his congregation and other churches in the Connecticut River Valley.

To be sure, and Edwards would certainly not discount this, God does work in surprising times and we may very well point to times of personal revival and even times of revival on a larger scale. Ultimately, however, the race is not best run in fits and spurts. It's a matter of patiently running the whole course, of slowly and steadily realizing the wonderful mercy and infinite grace of God at work in our lives and then not hoarding up these things for ourselves in a selfish and ungrateful way, but rather allowing our lives to be living testimonies to the surprising work of God.

## Note on the Sources

The first London edition of *A Faithful Narrative,* edited by Isaac Watts and John Guyse, appears in the Hickman edition of *The Works of Jonathan Edwards* (1834/1974), 1:344–64. *A Faithful Narrative* may also be found in *Jonathan Edwards on Revival* (1984). A portion of the work, including the introduction and the account of Abigail Hutchinson, appears in *A Jonathan Edwards Reader* (1995), pages 57–87. The authoritative text, based on Edwards's personal notes on his copies of the Guyse and Watts edition and the Boston edition, may be found in C. C. Goen's *The Great Awakening* (1972), volume 4 of the Yale edition of *The Works of Jonathan Edwards,* pages 97–211. Goen also reprints the original letter Edwards sent to Colman, Colman's abridgment of the letter that was published in Boston, and prefaces to various published editions. Goen's introduction also provides a lengthy discussion of both *A Faithful Narrative* and the revivals and the Great Awakening (pp. 1–94).

# 5

# OF METEORS AND STARS
## A Treatise Concerning Religious Affections

*One sure test of any thinker is the courage and
persistence he displays in attacking fundamental
questions. Judged by this criterion, Edwards was a
thinker of stature.*
—John E. Smith

*It is doubtless true, and evident from these Scriptures,
that the essence of all true religion lies in holy love.*
—Jonathan Edwards

A*Treatise Concerning Religious Affections* is the kind
of book that transcends its own generation. It is,
in every sense of the label, a classic, a literary and
theological masterpiece. The book earns this label because
it addresses numerous problems that, generation after generation, plague Christians and the church.

One such problem that perennially trips up the church
involves the head and the heart. Bringing these two together
challenges and confounds all of us. Even Paul addresses this
issue by exploring the relationship between zeal and knowl-

edge. Either one without the other results in problems—a warped spirituality and a distorted view of living the Christian life. Like a pendulum, the tendency to move from one to the other typifies individual Christians, entire churches, and sometimes entire generations of the church.

The question of the relationship between the head and the heart, however, is not Edwards's main aim in this book. Rather, he focuses on what he thinks to be the second most fundamental question that anyone can ask. Edwards's disciple and close companion Joseph Bellamy wrote a book entitled *True Religion Delineated* in 1750. Bellamy asked his mentor to write the preface. Edwards agreed and penned these words:

> The Being of God is reckoned the first, greatest and most fundamental of all things that are the objects of knowledge or belief. And next to that must be reckoned the nature of that religion which God requires of us, and must be found in us, in order to our enjoying the benefits of God's favor: or rather this may be esteemed of like importance with the other; for it in like manner concerns us to know how we may honor and please God, and be accepted of him, as it concerns us to know that he has a being.
>
> This is the point of infinite consequence to every single person; each one having to do with God as his supreme judge, who will fix his eternal state, according as he finds him to be with or without true religion. And this is also a point that vastly concerns the public interests of the church of God.

### Edwards's Mite

Four years earlier Edwards had put forth his own answer to this fundamental question in his *Treatise Concerning Religious Affections*. He rather humbly refers to this work as his "mite" in which he employs his "best (however feeble) ef-

THE

# TREATISE

ON

# RELIGIOUS AFFECTIONS,

BY THE LATE

REV. JONATHAN EDWARDS, A. M.

SOMEWHAT ABRIDGED.

———◦—◦◊◊◦—◦———

PUBLISHED BY THE

AMERICAN TRACT SOCIETY,

NO. 150 NASSAU-STREET, NEW-YORK.

• • • • • • • • •

D Fanshaw, Printer.

By far one of Edwards's most popular works, *Religious Affections* enjoyed numerous reprints, though often, as with this edition from the early 1800s, in an abridged format.

forts." These efforts are directed at the questions related to genuine religious experience. Such questions include: How does one know that a given work is indeed a work of the Holy Spirit? Or, how can one distinguish between a true believer and a hypocrite? Or, as Edwards himself asks in the preface to his book, "What is the nature of true religion?"

He realizes that many others have wrestled with this question, yet these attempts often attract more heat than light and tend to raise confusion rather than clear the air. But Edwards will not let the question go. In fact, he notes that since beginning his studies in theology, he has engaged this question "with the utmost diligence and care." And *Religious Affections* is the fruit of his decades of reflection.

He gets at this fundamental question by focusing our attention on the *affections*. On the one hand, using this term was a wise move. On the other, it was a dangerous move. Using this term makes Edwards's thought susceptible to misinterpretation and abuse, despite his efforts to safeguard it.

One reason Edwards's thought on the affections gets misinterpreted concerns the sheer popularity of the book. John Wesley and others were so impressed by Edwards's treatise that they reproduced and distributed tens of thousands of copies. Between 1833 and 1875, the American Tract Society alone distributed 75,000 copies. The only problem is that these editions were abridged and stripped of the careful theological framework and logical argumentation undergirding the text.

Even the American philosopher and psychologist William James relied upon Edwards's *Religious Affections* in his own classic text, *Varieties of Religious Experience*. But he was using an abridged edition, and even then he used it quite selectively. James takes Edwards to be doing nothing more than establishing one's subjective experience as that which gives shape and meaning to religion and religious truth.

In more recent times, advocates of the Toronto Blessing have appealed to Edwards in order to gain credibility and to justify their extreme behavior. Milder examples of the misuses and abuse of Edwards's thought also abound. From the early 1800s to the present, those who take revival fervor as the evidence of a true work of God often claim Edwards as their spiritual father.

Edwards, to be sure, would not recognize himself in William James's account of his work, nor would he appreciate his writings being used to vindicate the Toronto Blessing, and he would not be impressed by the generations of revivalists who call him father. In fact, the views represented by these groups and the dangers they present are precisely why he wrote *Religious Affections*. In the unabridged edition, Edwards presents a thorough and challenging argument. He develops his argument in three parts, asking and answering three questions: What is an affection? What are not genuine signs? What are genuine signs? A summary of each part follows below.

## What Is an Affection?

Clerics, laity, and theologians alike have wrestled with the question of the relationship between the head and the heart. Perhaps you have heard the saying, "There are twelve inches between heaven and hell—the difference between the head and the heart." The transparent point is that a mere head knowledge is inadequate; one must believe with the heart. This disjuncture, so prevalent in the thinking of many today, offers no real solution to the challenge of understanding what constitutes true religious knowledge or a genuine religious experience of conversion. Edwards offers a real solution to this impasse with his concept of affections.

I mentioned above that this was a dangerous move on the part of Edwards because it risks misunderstanding and distortion. That indeed occurred, and it continues to occur. To avoid misunderstanding Edwards, it's better to start with what the affections are not before laying out what they are.

Edwards did not intend for the affections to be equated with emotions. In fact, he repudiates emotional experiences as any true sign of genuine religious affections. Second, the designation of affections is not to be taken as an experience. While it is true that Edwards speaks of religious experiences, it is not true that this is what he means by the affections. Finally, we should not read the affections as pointing to some type of a mystical sense, or a sixth sense, that transcends ordinary knowledge and ordinary experiences. Despite Edwards's efforts to safeguard his thought and to avoid such misreadings, these three ways are often the way that the affections are interpreted.

But, if this is not what Edwards means by the affections, then we are still faced with the task of defining them positively. To do this, it's helpful to set Edwards in his historical context and read his work against the backdrop of John Locke. Among the many ideas of John Locke that intrigued the New England minister, as well as the European and New England community, stands Locke's notion of the *faculty psychology*.

This idea views the self as made of various aspects, which Locke refers to as "faculties." These aspects include such things as the soul, intellect, and physicality. These are the parts of human nature, and Locke viewed them as distinct and even conflicting. Our contemporary head-versus-heart debates are a distant descendant of this idea. Edwards viewed faculty psychology as detrimental and countered by enlisting the idea of the affections.

He does, however, borrow from Locke the idea that the soul consists of both the *understanding* and what he refers to as *inclination*. These could also be referred to as the intellect and will. Edwards then takes us a step further to analyze what drives these faculties. Underlying the will, he argues, is the almost universal and perennial notion of the *heart*. But, contrary to a fragmented view of the self, which usually follows from this train of thought, Edwards proposes a unified view of the self by looking beyond the heart to the *affections*.

Everybody, he reasoned, has affections. Motivating our actions, they drive all that we do. They both draw us to that which we approve of and like, and pull us back from that which we disapprove of and dislike. Edwards describes the affections this way: "The affections are of two sorts: they are those by which the soul is carried out to what is in view, cleaving to it or seeking it; or those by which it is averse from it and opposes it." Although the affections lie beneath the surface, they continually make their presence felt in both our thoughts and actions. Like a ship's rudder, they orient our lives.

Applying this to conversion, one can see that the affections bring together both the understanding or knowledge and the will or inclination. Conversion is not so much experiencing Christ as it is knowing Christ. Yet, this knowledge is not about mere facts. Edwards develops this idea fully in his sermon on Hebrews 5:12 entitled "Importance and Advantage of a Thorough Knowledge of Divine Truth."

Here he distinguishes between notional and spiritual knowledge. He is not distinguishing two types of knowledge. Rather, he is distinguishing different relationships that one may have to knowledge. To illustrate this, if one has notional knowledge, then one knows the propositions of the gospel or has a knowledge of God and Christ's work and sin, much as one knows a phone number or today's date. If, however, one has a spiritual knowledge of the gospel, then one is inclined to it, relishes it, and sees it in all of its beauty, harmony, and excellency. In other words, Edwards brings together zeal and knowledge, or the heart and the head.

The affections also function like a watermark; when examined they reveal our true identity. And holding up the affections to the light becomes Edwards's primary concern in *Religious Affections*. In fact, he proceeds to hold up numerous actions—twenty-four, to be exact—to the light in order to get a good look at the watermark. Edwards examines the first twelve actions in an attempt to show that they are not evidence of genuine religious affections. These constitute what he refers to as "no certain signs."

## No Certain Signs

How can you identify a hypocrite? How can you be discerning about your own experiences? These two questions comprise the deepest concerns of the Puritans. Hypocrisy and self-deception stand next to Arminianism and deism as the Puritan's most feared challenges. Edwards addresses these two concerns through the backdoor by pointing out that what we often take to be genuine affections do not in fact guarantee genuine religious affections.

He is not looking at all of these twelve signs as something to avoid. He expresses concern, however, over a few of them and would strongly counsel that these certain ones be avoided. Nevertheless, the presence of any of these signs does not demand that they flow from and give evidence of a genuine conversion or a genuine work of God in one's life. Grasping his logic here reveals his true point in this part of the book. These twelve signs under consideration do not necessarily guarantee genuine religious affections, and we should be cautious about using them as certain evidence.

Edwards's caution on these points serves well to give us pause in evaluating our own selves as well as others. Just as

John Bunyan's Pilgrim experienced a series of interviews before being granted entrance into the Palace Beautiful, Bunyan's allegorical designation of the church, so, too, Edwards here stresses a crucial element of Puritanism: examination. Bunyan, Edwards, and other Puritans were intent on examining both their own lives, due to the powers of self-deception, and the lives of others, due to the subtleties of hypocrisy.

It is important to keep both examinations in mind. I suspect there is a tendency in reading this section of *Religious Affections* to miss Edwards's emphasis on self-examination. It's rather easy to identify these twelve signs in others and quickly congratulate ourselves for avoiding such snares of religiosity. It's like listening to a sermon and thinking of how well it applies to so many others. Hearing sermons for the sake of others, or reading *Religious Affections* for the sake of others, however, misses the point. It is one thing to put someone else under the magnifying glass; it is quite another to turn the glass on ourselves, and doing so with the help of Edwards in this section of his book can be a painful but worthwhile experience.

A few of his particular concerns well illustrate his overall aim regarding these no certain signs. His third sign concerns religious talk. He writes, "It is no sign that affections are truly gracious, or that they are not, that they cause those who have them, to be fluent, fervent, and abundant in talking of religious things." Edwards concedes that such actions do arise from genuine religious affections, but not necessarily so. Quoting Jude, Edwards likens such religious talk to great clouds without water. Although they appear to be full of water, they "seldom afford much rain to the dry and thirsty earth." "It is the nature of false religion," he continues, "to affect show and observation." As William Shakespeare's Gertrude tells Hamlet, "The lady protests too much, methinks."

His eighth sign concerns what has come to be called a morphology of conversion. The word *morphology* refers to a form or a pattern. In this context, the full meaning is that of a set pattern of conversion, or the following of a certain order. The Puritans expected and looked for certain responses and actions in individuals undergoing conversion. Typically, these responses followed a pattern. At first there may be indifference to the gospel, but once the reality sinks in, a deep and intense sense of sin and impending judgment follows. This in turn brings about a sense of hopelessness and even despair which allows one to see his or her need for Christ. This then is followed by a sense of joy and comfort. While today's morphology might look quite different, especially in some circles, a discerning examination will probably reveal patterns of conversion experiences.

Edwards argues that exhibiting these patterns—even if the order is to a "T"—does not guarantee genuine religious affections. He expresses his point this way: "Nothing can certainly be determined concerning the nature of the affections by this, that comforts and joys seem to follow convictions in a certain order." He further notes that "no order or method of operations and experiences, is any certain sign of their divinity."

His reasoning entails the point that Scripture, while mentioning the gracious and saving operations of God numerous times, does not give a certain method or order. He concludes that since we don't find an order in Scripture, we shouldn't look for one. As he observes, "[It] should be enough with Christians, who are willing to have the Word of God, rather than their own philosophy, and experiences, and conjectures, as their sufficient and sure guide in things of this nature."

FIG. 5.2

## Signs of Genuine Religious Affections

| No Certain Signs | Certain Signs |
|---|---|
| 1  Great deal of religious zeal or fervor | Genuine source: the affections are spiritual, supernatural, and divine |
| 2  Effects on the body (physical manifestations) | Delight in divine things not for self-interest |
| 3  Talking about religion | Love of divine things for their inherent beauty and excellency |
| 4  Source other than self | Illumination: rightly understanding divine things |
| 5  Ability to recite Scripture | Assurance: conviction of the reality and certainty of divine things |
| 6  The appearance of love | Humiliation: a sense of insufficiency and unworthiness |
| 7  Multiple and various affections | Transformation: change of nature |
| 8  Affections follow a pattern | Christlikeness: promote love, meekness, quietness, forgiveness, and mercy, as well as boldness and zeal |
| 9  Devoting much time to religion and zealous in worship | Sensitivity: a tender, not a hardened heart |
| 10  Praising and glorifying God in speech | Symmetry and proportion: reflecting the whole image of Christ, not a disproportion of the affections |
| 11  Self-confidence in religious experience | Spiritual hunger: desiring the self and sin less and spiritual growth more |
| 12  Outward signs that convince even the saints | Bearing fruit: the manifestation of Christianity as the business of life |

Finally, his twelfth and last negative sign concerns outward actions that convince even the saints. Edwards puts the matter rather succinctly: "The true saints have not such a spirit of discerning, that they can certainly determine who are godly, and who are not." It is impossible, he notes, to see into the heart. Of course, Edwards exclaims, "When there are many probable appearances of piety in others, it is the duty of the saints to receive them cordially into their charity, to love, and to rejoice in them, as their brother in Christ." He is not calling for an attitude of suspicion as much as he is simply reminding his readers of the difference between professing Christ and possessing Christ.

Edwards, however, is not content with simply telling the story of what does not count as evidence of genuine religious affections. He wants to offer some positive points not only to discern genuine religious affections, but also to encourage them. Here, too, he offers twelve signs, although he devotes significantly more space to this, the third and final part of his treatise.

**Distinguishing Signs**

We typically get in trouble for reading the end of a book first. In this case, however, it would help. In the twelfth and final sign, Edwards reveals what he refers to as the chief sign. In fact, he reorients the previous signs of truly gracious affections to the notion of practice. In other words, in the last sign he looks for the manifestation of the earlier eleven signs in one's life.

Sometimes we distinguish between professing and possessing Christ. This is both a helpful and legitimate construct, as we have seen in this chapter. Edwards would make the point that while this is a valid construct, it can be improved upon. According to Edwards, a given profession is true if and only if it is *possession as evidenced in practice*. His twelfth sign essentially expounds upon Christ's own words, "By your fruits, you will know them."

Before we go any further, however, it might be helpful to return to some of the earlier signs in this section. The first few signs all reference the divine origin and nature of genuine religious affections. Edwards expresses this in the first sign, declaring that "affections that are truly spiritual and gracious, arise from those influences and operations on the heart, which are spiritual, supernatural, and divine."

On the surface, this argument begs the question. If an affection is genuine because it is spiritual, then how can one know that it is spiritual? How Edwards proceeds to develop this point, however, explains what he is doing here. Obviously, genuine religious affections would come only from the Holy Spirit, and only the Spirit enables one to know that the gospel is in fact true and real. This in effect means that true religious affections are based upon the regeneration and renewal of the Holy Spirit.

Those without the Spirit of God are incapable of producing genuine religious affections because, following Paul in 1 Corinthians 2, Edwards argues they are natural and not spiritual. He then explains the implications:

> Those gracious influences which the saints are subject of, and the effects of God's Spirit which they experience, are entirely above nature, altogether of a different kind from anything that men find within themselves by nature, or only in the exercise of natural principles.

Consequently, he concludes that "gracious affections are from those influences that are supernatural." This leads Edwards to discuss the concept of the Spirit's witness and the doctrine of assurance. Edwards devotes a great deal of time to this concept in part 3, demonstrating that the Spirit's witness is a certain sign. Although the doctrine of assurance is plainly taught in Scripture, it is often misunderstood and confused. By the witness of the Spirit, Edwards does not intend some vague and ambiguous "having the Spirit." Neither does he infer that outward manifestations attest to this inner witness of the Spirit. To understand Edwards's meaning here, we need to set his teaching in the broader context of the Puritan understanding of assurance.

Going back to John Calvin, we learn that the Spirit works with the Word. That is to say that the Spirit works through the written Word of Scripture. This work takes on a lively and dynamic character as the Spirit opens one's eyes to the truth of the gospel, enables one to see its beauty and truthfulness, and then assures one that he or she is in fact God's child. Edwards expresses this idea in a two-step process in the fourth and fifth signs in part 3. The fourth sign declares, "Gracious Affections do arise from the mind's being enlightened rightly and spiritually to understand or apprehend divine things." Here Edwards relates how, through the Spirit's work of regeneration, we are given a spiritual understanding and ability to see Scripture accurately.

Edwards expresses this as a whole new outlook not only on Scripture, but on God, the self, and the world. And, it's not just a new way of seeing, it is a new way of living or a new disposition. This is Edwards's notion of the new sense, which is not a sixth sense, but a complete overhaul of the self, resulting in a new creation. Edwards describes it as a "new sense of the heart," a new sense of "the supreme beauty and sweetness of the holiness or moral perfection of divine things, together with all that discerning and knowledge of things of religion, that depends upon and flows from such a sense." And, as Edwards concludes, "When the true beauty and amiableness of the holiness or true moral good that is in divine things, is discovered to the soul, it as it were opens a new world to its view."

This new sense leads to the second step of understanding the Spirit's work as Edwards unfolds it in the fifth sign. Here the certain sign of genuine religious affections consists in the notion that they "are attended with a reasonable and spiritual conviction of the judgment, of the reality and certainty of divine things." This is the doctrine of assurance. Edwards continues to describe it as "a conviction and persuasion of the truth of the things of the gospel, and sight of their evidence and reality, as the Scriptures speak of." Such a conviction of truth is lost on those without the Spirit. Consequently, assurance becomes a certain sign because it is a work that only the Spirit can produce.

But Edwards reserves his chief certain sign for last. He succinctly states the twelfth sign: "Gracious and holy affections have their exercise and fruit in Christian practice." This leads him to discuss the doctrine of perseverance and the natural process of growth and bearing fruit that accompanies genuine conversion. He does acknowledge that the saints may not always live saintly lives. In fact, he writes:

> True saints may be guilty of some kinds and degrees of backsliding, may be foiled by particular temptations, and fall into sin, yea, great sins; but they can never fall away so as to grow weary of religion and the service of God, and to habitually dislike and neglect it, either on its own account or on account of the difficulties that attend it.

But, if people truly have the Spirit, then they will evidence it in their lives. He proceeds in this last sign to relate all of the previous signs to this great truth. He refers to the direct tendency or connection between this sign and the other signs, noting that practicing holiness is what living the

Christian life is all about. He writes, "True grace is not an inactive thing; there is nothing in heaven or earth of a more active nature; for it is life itself." He then adds, "Godliness in the heart has a direct relation to practice as a fountain does to a stream, or as the luminous nature of the sun has to beams sent forth, or as life has to breathing."

Bearing fruit is a sign for others. As Edwards remarks, "Christian practice or holy life, is a manifestation and sign of the sincerity of a professing Christian to the eye of his neighbors and brethren." In this, we hear echoes of Christ's words, "By their fruit you will recognize them" (Matt. 7:16). Bearing fruit, however, is also a sign for one's own conscience, and on this point Edwards concludes his treatise. "Christian practice," he observes, "is a distinguishing and sure evidence of grace to persons' own consciences." As James teaches, our works justify and demonstrate our faith (James 2:20–24). So Edwards concludes, "Christian practice is the chief of all the signs of saving grace."

## Meteors and Stars

Edwards typically turns to nature in order to gain a deeper understanding of God's will and his work in accomplishing his grand purpose of redemption. He also finds nature to be a perfect illustrator. And he uses nature's illustrations to guide others in understanding God's ways. In *Religious Affections* he looks to the sky, referring to the distinction between stars and comets. Extending his metaphor to stars and meteors might help capture the distinction that he drew between genuine and spurious religious affections in this classic work.

A meteor, although it can put on quite a show, is short-lived. No sooner does it ignite and display its radiance than it self-destructs. Such is the case for the hypocrite. Or, for that matter, the illustration also extends to religious zeal not built upon or anchored in the solid ground of the genuine work of the Holy Spirit. On the other hand, stars shine consistently and for the ages through a self-generating power source. Indeed, they lack the momentary thrill of the meteor. But what they lack they make up in spades through their continual, brilliant display.

Putting *Religious Affections* in its historical context further serves to drive home this point. This book stands as perhaps Edwards's last and decidedly most mature formal writing on the aftermath of the revivals and the issues surrounding conversion. While much of his thought here coincides with his earlier treatments, such as his emphasis on the Spirit's work of assurance and his stress on the new sense, here he expands his understanding to place equal emphasis on the sanctified life that follows as proof and evidence of a genuine work of conversion.

*Religious Affections,* to be sure, challenges its readers. In the preface to his edition, John Wesley referred to Edwards's heaping together of "so many curious subtle, metaphysical distinctions, as are sufficient to puzzle the brains, and confound the intellect." Indeed, the complexities and subtleties of his reasoning and argument may not come easily and some paragraphs warrant a few readings. Nevertheless, his underlying point is clear: true religion consists in holy affections that are grounded upon the work of the Spirit in conversion, result in assurance of salvation, and evidence themselves throughout one's life in love and holiness.

While it contains rigorous arguments, it should be remembered that this book originally consisted of sermons aimed not at academic debates, but at helping Christians to be discerning about their own religious experiences, as well as those of others. And, Edwards intended both the sermons and the book not simply to help evaluate affections, but also to encourage the manifestation of genuine religious affections.

In one of the most interesting selections from the first part of the book, Edwards declares, "That religion which God requires, and will accept, does not consist in weak, dull and lifeless *wouldings*, raising us but a little above a state of indifference. God, in his word, greatly insists upon it, that we be in good earnest, fervent in spirit, and our hearts vigorously engaged in religion." *Wouldings* is Edwards's own term. Some editions of this work insert the word *wishes* in its place. I prefer his term, even though it is not a word and is quirky and cumbersome. It is not enough to say that I would believe if, or I would do a certain action if, or I would say a certain thing if. In this case *would* is not good enough.

True religion, Edwards notes, is a "powerful thing" that works itself out not in what one would do, or, for that matter, in what one should do. Rather, true religion is one's thought, speech, and action. In short, it is one's life. And that, Edwards argues, is a certain sign of genuine religious affections.

### Note on the Sources

*A Treatise Concerning Religious Affections* is available in a number of editions. An authoritative edition, coupled with a lengthy introduction, is John E. Smith's *Religious Affections* (1959), volume 2 in the Yale edition of *The Works of Jonathan Edwards*. The treatise is also available in the Hickman edition of *The Works of Jonathan Edwards* (1834/1974), 1:234–343. The Banner of Truth also publishes a standalone edition, *The Religious Affections* (1986).

*6*

# VISIBLE SAINTS
## *An Humble Inquiry*

The Northampton Church record leaves much untold when it simply reads "June 22, 1750 Revd Jonathan Edwards was dismissed." As discussed in chapter 2, the controversy between Edwards and Northampton centered around the Lord's Supper and involves the long shadow cast by his venerable predecessor and grandfather, Solomon Stoddard. To understand the story, however, we need to go back even further than Solomon Stoddard and take a hard look at Puritanism.

Although this is a rough assessment, the word *Puritan* reveals the quest of those who wear the label. That is to say that the Puritans were about being *pure*. For the most part, historians and popular culture alike view this notion and this quest pejoratively and capitalize upon it to caricature the Puritans as frowning, stodgy killjoys just waiting to catch somebody in the act. While the Puritans desired a life of holiness, to be sure, this caricature is overdrawn and misleading. The Puritans embraced life, establishing cultural and educational institutions that have continuing impact on American and Western culture—all the while taking seriously the catechism's exhortation to glorify and *enjoy* God with their whole beings.

But living a pure life tells only part of the story. The Puritans, and this goes back to their founding in Old England, sought a pure church. Such a church, in their words, requires *visible saints*. One British historian captures the essence of this concept when he refers to the Puritan church as a serious religious club for serious religious athletes, not a social club for half-hearted and occasional participants. Visible saints both profess Christ and evidence him through their lives. In one of his earlier *Miscellanies* writings, Edwards offers his definition of this Puritan concept:

> By VISIBLE CHRISTIANS must be meant being Christians in what is visible, or in what appears, or in what is outward. To be a Christian really is to have faith and holiness and obedience of heart. To be outwardly a Christian is to have outward faith, that is profession of faith, and outward holiness in the visible life and conversation.

The question arises, of course, as to how you can identify a visible Christian. We have already seen in the previous chapter that Edwards challenged the outward manifestations that typically count for genuine religious affections. There he argued that such signs may in fact not be any certain evidence of a genuine work of God in conversion. That being the case, how can you tell a saint when you see one? What signs alert you to one's spiritual condition? A recent cartoon pictures a young person bedecked in a Christian T-shirt, jewelry, and accessories, with this caption, "They'll know we are Christians by our *trinkets*." If we could bring Edwards forward a few centuries, he might well say that putting a bumper sticker on your car or wearing a particular bracelet is no certain sign.

So the problem persists. How do you know a saint when you see one? This question can be aimed at Reverend Edwards and, for that matter, at pastors today when someone comes seeking membership in the church. In Edwards's day his question of visible sainthood also related to admission to the Lord's Supper. This was a rather complex and quite personal issue for Edwards, and as we have pointed out, it cost him his position as minister at Northampton.

## The Communion Controversy

Understanding Edwards's dismissal involves not only the notion of visible saints, but also the shadow of Solomon Stoddard looming over Northampton. Stoddard's teaching on this issue was so well known that it came to be called Stoddardeanism. This position is also referred to as the halfway covenant, and it modified church membership qualifications by allowing those who had been baptized as infants, even though unregenerate as adults, to present their own children to the church for baptism. The issue at Northampton, however, had more to do with admission to the Lord's Supper than with baptism. Stoddard eliminated regeneration as necessary for admission to communion, and published his views in two widely distributed works in the early 1700s.

Stoddard viewed communion as a "converting ordinance." Rather than restrict communion to those who had publicly professed Christ and were visible saints, Stoddard opened communion to anyone who desired to participate and who had been baptized as an infant, hoping that through partaking of communion they would come to Christ. He was not, however, without his challengers. Fellow New England minister and colonial poet Edward Taylor devoted a great deal of energy to refuting Stoddard's position. Taylor even took to verse:

> This bread and wine begets no Souls; but is set
> 'Fore spiritual life to feed the Same.
> This Feast is no Regenerating fare.
> But food for those Regenerate that are.

And then there is Stoddard's other critic, his assistant and grandson, Jonathan Edwards. By Edwards's own admission he did not agree with Stoddard's position almost from the beginning. Edwards was not, however, in a position to challenge his grandfather. He even waited for some time to put his own views regarding the Lord's Supper into practice at Northampton. Rather than seeing communion as a converting ordinance, Edwards agreed with Taylor and sought to restrict participation to visible saints. What finally prompted Edwards to enforce this view was the same phenomenon that prompted the writing of *Religious Affections*. Edwards was deeply troubled by the temporary and shallow response of the Great Awakening, and he feared that relaxed standards for admission to the Lord's Supper only further contributed to the problem and led to an unconverted congregation.

Edwards's position was rather simple. In order to come to the table of the Lord's Supper, he argued, one must be a *full* member of the church, a visible saint. This new teaching from the pulpit at Northampton was not well received by the leadership of the church. They came to Edwards and asked him to write a defense of his position. The result is the book published in 1749 with the lengthy title, *An Humble Inquiry into the Rules of the Word of God Concerning the Qualifications Requisite to a Compleat Standing and Full Communion in the Visible Christian Church.*

In the preface to his book, Edwards expresses his reluctance to announce his disagreement with Stoddard. He first notes that at one time he held to Stoddard's position, "though never without some difficulties in my view, which I could not solve." He continues:

> Yet, however, a distrust of my own understanding and deference to the authority of so venerable a man, the seeming strength of his arguments, together with the success he had in ministry, and his great reputation and influence, prevailed for a long time to bear down my scruples. But the difficulties and uneasiness on my mind increasing, as I became more studied in divinity, and as I improved in experience, this brought me to closer diligence and care to search the scriptures, and more impartially to examine and weigh the arguments of my grandfather, and such other authors as I could get on his side of the question. By which means after long searching, pondering, viewing, and reviewing, I gained satisfaction, became fully settled in the opinion I now maintain, as in this discourse here offered for public view; and dared to proceed no further in a practice and administration herewith.

Arriving at such a position and expressing it in both the pulpit and the press not only required a great deal of time and searching by Edwards, but also was something he was quite reluctant to do. Again, Edwards notes:

> It is far from a pleasing circumstance of this publication, that it is against what my honoured grandfather strenuously maintained. . . . I can truly say, on account of this and some other considerations, it is what I engage in with the greatest reluctance that I ever undertook any public service in my life.

As reluctant as he was, and as distasteful as the prospects were, nevertheless he was compelled to write this book. He explains the reason in a veiled reference:

> I have been brought to this necessity in divine providence, by such a situation of affairs and coincidence of circumstances and events, as I choose at present to be silent about; and which is not needful, nor perhaps expedient, for me to publish to the world.

A group of Bostonian ministers identified as "His American Friends" also joined Edwards in writing a preface to this work. They are not so discreet, however, in referencing the extenuating circumstances of the book. Their preface concludes with the following:

> We heartily pray that the reverend Author and his flock may for a long time be happy together; that their cordial love and tenderness to each other may continue and operate in mutual and all lawful condescensions and forbearances under different sentiments in these particulars.

They wrote these words in August 1749. In less than one year the peaceful and happy relationship that they prayed for failed to materialize, as leaders of the Northampton church were not convinced by Edwards's argument and dismissed him. Even after his dismissal from Northampton, the controversy continued. Solomon Williams, Edwards's cousin and a Stoddard devotee, published a reply to Edwards's *Humble Inquiry* in 1751.

Edwards utilized the same Boston publisher and printed a response the next year. He affixed a title that clearly reveals his assessment of Williams's book, as it declares, *Misrepresentations Corrected and the Truth Vindicated*. The publisher also printed a letter from Edwards to his

FIG. 6.1

**Writings on the Communion Controversy**

1749    *An Humble Inquiry . . . Concerning the Qualifications Requisite
        to . . . Full Communion*

1752    *Misrepresentations Corrected and the Truth Vindicated: A
        Reply to Solomon Williams' "The True State of the Question
        Concerning Qualifications for Communion"*

1750s   *Narrative of the Communion Controversy*

Northampton congregation. The letter goes a long way in explaining Edwards's aim throughout the whole controversy. It also shows how deeply he cared for his flock even though he was no longer their minister. He begins his letter by making the following point:

> Though I am not now your pastor, yet having stood so long in that relation to you, I look on myself obliged, notwithstanding as of late all that has passed between us, still to maintain a special concern for your spiritual welfare. And as your present circumstances appear to me very evidently attended with some peculiar dangers, threatening the great wounding of the interest of vital religion among you . . .

He continues in the letter to make specific responses to Solomon Williams's book in an attempt to help the congregation see the consequences of Williams's position for "vital religion." The sum of Edwards's reply concerns Williams's sole requirement for admission to the Lord's Supper: moral sincerity. This moved far beyond Stoddard's position and the implications of it startled Edwards. He consequently concludes his letter by warning his former congregation of the danger: "I beseech you, brethren, seasonably to consider how dark is the cloud that hangs over you, and how melancholy the prospect (especially with regard to the rising generation) in many respects."

Edwards, however, managed to engage this entire controversy in such a way as not to leave behind simply a series of polemical texts, but to make a lasting positive contribution that extends beyond the church doors at Northampton to reach those rising generations. In the following section of this chapter we will briefly look at Edwards's teaching in the first of his writings on the communion controversy, *An Humble Inquiry.*

## Complete Standing

Edwards divides this work into three parts, and like many of his treatises, it is replete with thoroughly developed series of arguments. The whole treatise hinges upon the idea that only church members in complete standing should be admitted to the Lord's Supper and to the full privileges of church membership. He takes the first part of the book to present this thesis and to clarify his terms. In the second part he offers his reasons for his position and engages many of the ideas of Stoddard in the process. Finally, he raises and answers twenty various objections to his position in the third part. These objections include biblical references, theological issues, and arguments from experience.

Visible saints, Edwards argues, evidence saving grace. He observes that "saintship, godliness, and holiness, of which, according to Scripture, professing Christians and visible saints do make a profession and have a visibility, is not any religion and virtue that is the result of common grace, or moral sincerity (as it is called) but saving grace." Consequently, visible sainthood stands as the only requirement for admission to communion. Edwards bases this on the examples given of the early church in Acts and also on the teaching of the epistles. He concludes his arguments from Scripture by noting, "The Scriptures represent the visible church of Christ, as a society having its several members united by the bond of Christian brotherly love."

Edwards, of course, needs to connect this idea of visible sainthood as requisite for membership in the church to admission to communion. This is precisely what he does next. He looks to 1 Corinthians 11:28. He concludes his discussion of this with the following:

> When therefore the apostle exhorts to *self-examination* as a preparative for the sacramental supper, he may well be understood to put professors upon inquiring whether they have such a principle of *faith*, by means whereof they are habitually in a capacity and disposition of mind to *discern the Lord's body*, practically and spiritually, (as well as speculatively and notionally) in their communicating at the Lord's table: which is what none can do who have a faith short of that which is justifying and saving. It is only a living faith that capacitates men to *discern the Lord's body* in the sacrament with that spiritual sensation or spiritual gust, which is suitable to the nature and design of the ordinance, and which the apostle seems principally to intend.

In other words, the reality of communion is only known to those who know of the reality of Christ and of saving faith. And only those who have such faith should be admitted to the Lord's table. But there are objections to this position and Edwards did not dodge them. As mentioned above, he treats objections to his view in part 3 of the book. Some objections center around one's ability to know that he or she is a visible saint. In other words, these objections involve the doctrine of assurance. The tenth objection addresses this directly. Edwards words the objection this way:

The natural consequence of the doctrine which has been maintained, is the bringing multitudes of persons of a tender conscience and true piety into great perplexities; who being at a loss about the state of their souls, must needs be as much in suspense about their duty.

Edwards replies by noting that even "Mr. Stoddard often taught his people, that assurance is attainable and that those who are true saints might know it if they would; that is, if they would use proper means and endeavors in order to [know] it." In fact, Edwards views the communion table as one of those proper means.

True saints are given to times of perplexity or doubt about their spiritual state. Usually, as Edwards notes, this is due to their own sin and neglect of attending to God's Word and to communion. He teaches that God's people would "on every return of the Lord's supper" put themselves on "the strictest examination and trial of the state of their souls, agreeable to that rule of the apostle, 1 Cor. 11:28." He then observes, "The neglect of which great duty of frequent and thorough self-examination, seems to be one main cause of the darkness and perplexity of the saints, and the reason why they have so little comfort in ordinances, and so little comfort in general."

Christians, Edwards observes, can know with certainty that they are in fact in Christ. That certainty comes from the Holy Spirit. Assurance, however, can, as the Westminster Confession states, wax and wane. Edwards helps us to see that attending communion and following Paul's injunction to self-examination does not diminish or jeopardize assurance. Rather, it is one of those means that God intends to give assurance and along with it comfort.

Another objection also raises a practical matter. This objection states, "You cannot keep out hypocrites, when all is said and done." Edwards concedes that such may be the case. He does not conclude from this, however, that his position is wrong or unscriptural. Throughout the work, he refers to this problem by drawing attention to the reality of hypocrites in the church. The visible church is, however unfortunately, comprised of both true saints and those professing to be saints, but not indeed saints. The early church was not without this problem either. Consequently, Edwards notes that this objection "is not so much an objection against the doctrine I am defending, as a reflection upon the Scripture itself, with regard to the rules it gives, either for persons to judge of their own state, or for others to form a charitable judgment, as if they were of little or no service."

One other objection represents those that address biblical issues. This particular one concerns Judas. The objection stands as the following:

> Christ himself administered the Lord's supper to Judas, whom he knew at the same time to be graceless; which is a full evidence, that grace is not in itself a requisite qualification in order to coming to the Lord's supper; and if it be not a requisite in itself, a profession of it cannot be requisite.

Edwards offers a detailed answer in which he first raises the question of whether or not Judas in fact participated in the Last Supper. He concludes, based on a reading of the text, that while Judas was there for the Passover meal, nothing in the text demands that he participated in the partaking of the cup and the bread that followed the meal. Nevertheless, Edwards grants that even if Judas did participate, his position still stands. He replies:

> Judas had made the same profession of regard to his master, and of forsaking all for him, as the other disciples: and therefore Christ did not openly renounce him till he himself

had destroyed his profession and visibility of saintship, by public scandalous apostasy. Supposing then the presence of Judas at the Lord's supper, this affords no consequence in favor of what I oppose.

Edwards ends his treatise by committing "this whole discourse (under God's blessing) to the reader's candid reflection and impartial judgment." He then adds:

> Having been fully persuaded in my own mind, as to what is the Scripture rule in this matter, after a most careful, painful, and long search, I am willing, in faithful prosecution of what appears to me of such importance and so plainly the mind and will of God, to resign to his providence, and leave the event in his hand.

As we know, the event did not have a very favorable outcome for Edwards in regards to his position at Northampton. Perhaps it is this resignation that enabled him to weather the storm of events that was to come in the ensuing months. In the earlier chapters relating to Edwards's biography, I mentioned that Edwards was no stranger to conflict throughout his ministry. In both these few words, as well as throughout the whole communion controversy, he models sound principles in dealing with conflict in the church.

## Sanctifying Grace

The Lord's Supper, the issue of the controversy, reminds us of both Christ's finished work on the cross and his work yet to be done in consummating his kingdom. It reminds us of the grace imparted at our salvation, converting us from children of darkness to children of light. It also impresses upon us the absolute dependence we continue to have upon the grace of God. Edwards captures all of these themes in his treatise on communion. He utilized a controversial and troubling situation to bring a sound and healthy teaching to a wide audience through his *Humble Inquiry*. Returning to Taylor's poem cited above, we find the true import of the Lord's Supper. In fact, both Taylor and Edwards remind us that communion, far from a perfunctory ritual, provides the nourishment of sanctifying grace for visible saints.

> Make Sanctifying Grace thrive every day,
> Making the spiritual man hate spiritual sloth
> And to abound in things of Holy growth.
>
> Lord, feed me with th' bread of thy Sacrament:
> And make me drink thy Sacramental Wine:
> That I may Grow by Graces nourishment
> Washed in thy Vinall liquor till I shine,
> And array'd in Sparkling Grace unto thy Glory,
> That so my life may be a gracious story.

## Note on the Sources

*An Humble Inquiry Concerning Qualifications for Communion* may be found in the Hickman edition of *The Works of Jonathan Edwards* (1834/1974), 1:431–84. *An Humble Inquiry* may also be found in David D. Hall's *Ecclesiastical Writings* (1994), volume 1 of the Yale edition of *The Works of Jonathan Edwards,* pages 165–348. His other writings on the communion controversy, including *Misrepresentations Corrected,* is also in these volumes. Hall's introduction (pp. 1–90) covers the history of the communion controversy in detail. For an accessible volume of the poetry of Edward Taylor, see *Early New England Meditative Poetry: Anne Bradstreet and Edward Taylor,* edited by Charles Hambrick-Stowe (New York: Paulist, 1988).

# PART 3

## WRITINGS ON THEOLOGY AND PHILOSOPHY

Throughout his life Edwards applied his mind to numerous subjects, and his efforts resulted in both published treatises that establish his reputation as America's foremost theologian-philosopher and numerous shorter writings in his various notebooks. In part 3 we examine both, beginning with his monumental, thirty-sermon series on the *History of the Work of Redemption*. Although he devoted some energy to preparing this text for publication, it was not published until after his death. We end with his defense of the Calvinistic understanding of divine sovereignty and human responsibility in *Freedom of the Will*, written during his years at Stockbridge.

In between we get a glimpse into Edwards's forays into science in some shorter writings regarding the revelation of God in nature. These texts reveal the breadth of Edwards's thought, as well as his ability to learn about God and his ways in all things, even spiders.

7

# God's Grand Scheme

*History of the Work of Redemption*

*My righteousness will last forever,*
*my salvation through all generations.*
 —Isaiah 51:8

*Tho' I long to see Mr. Edwards's refutation of the several*
*branches of Arminianism, yet I more long to see his*
*intended history of man's redemption. From such a pen*
*upon such a subject something highly valuable may be*
*expected.*
 —John Erskine to Joseph
 Bellamy, March 24, 1755

When the trustees of Princeton University called upon Edwards to be president, he hesitated. He thought that his algebra was rusty and that his demeanor was not suitable for the government of a college. He also viewed the long move from Massachusetts to New Jersey and the settling of his affairs as a rather grim and formidable prospect. But in his reply to the trustees he expressed his chief reluctance as the interruption in his studies, which he referred to as "the chief entertainment and delight of my life."

From before his student days his studies had occupied his free moments and managed to crowd out many other pursuits. When the letter from the trustees reached Edwards in 1757, he was anxious to see these thoughts materialize in print. In fact, he mentions a number of writing projects currently engaging his mind. One project in particular had been on his heart and mind for some time, a work he calls "A History of the Work of Redemption."

Edwards describes this work as a theology "in an entire new method, being thrown into the form of a history, considering the affair of Christian theology, as the whole of it, in each part, stands in reference to the great work of redemption by Jesus Christ." He considers this work of redemption "to be the grand design of all God's designs, and the *summum* and *ultimum* of all the divine operations and decrees; particularly considering all parts of the grand scheme in their historical order." He, however, never witnessed the realization of this dream.

Edwards poured a great deal of thought and energy into this project. He first preached a sermon series on this grand theme of redemption in 1739 between March and August. The sermons were preceded by numerous notebook entries in his *Miscellanies*. He returned to these notes and the sermons in the 1750s while at Stockbridge. Despite the considerable effort he applied to revising this material for publication, in the end he was unable to bring the manuscript to press.

Almost twenty years later, through the efforts of his son Jonathan Edwards Jr. and his longtime correspondent and friend, the Scottish minister John Erskine, an edition of *History of the Work of Redemption* appeared in Edinburgh in 1774. The Edinburgh edition went through numerous revisions, and in the 1790s first saw publication in Edwards's New England. Translations, including one in Arabic, and numerous editions abounded in the nineteenth century.

Consequently, this work stands among the most influential and widely regarded of Edwards's writings.

## Finding the Center

We can easily lose our way when navigating the Scriptures. The sixty-six books in all their variety present a challenge, especially to a new Christian. Consider also the rather grandiose question of what God is doing in this world. Or, you can put the matter this way: What is God accomplishing through history? These two issues, an overall understanding of Scripture and a philosophy of history, actually come together. They are the "center" of God's purpose for the world and are the center of the ever-elusive question of the meaning of life. Finding the answer to these questions is tantamount to making sense of life and of the world around us.

In his *History of the Work of Redemption* Edwards tackles both of these issues and finds the center to both Scripture and history in Christ. This principle goes a long way in understanding Edwards's thought. We might refer to it as *Christocentrism*, a rather cumbersome word that simply means that Christ is the center of all things. Edwards interprets Scripture on the basis of this principle, he organizes his system of theology around it, and he interprets and understands history in light of it.

Edwards learned this principle of Christocentrism in the pages of Scripture itself. Paul brings the concept to the fore in the opening verses of Ephesians as he explores the rich and manifold purpose and plan of God in redemption through Christ. Paul ends his lengthy sentence of verses 3–10 by observing that God has

> made known to us the mystery of his will according to his good pleasure, which he purposed in Christ, to be put into

Edwards first preached his series on the history of the work of redemption in 1739. He began his work on revising the sermons for publication in the 1750s, as evidenced in the title page from his manuscripts, although he was unable to finish the work.

effect when the times will have reached their fulfillment—to bring all things in heaven and earth together under one head, even Christ (Eph. 1:9–10).

# HISTORY

OF

# REDEMPTION,

ON A PLAN ENTIRELY ORIGINAL:

EXHIBITING THE

GRADUAL DISCOVERY AND ACCOMPLISHMENT OF THE

DIVINE PURPOSES

IN THE

## SALVATION OF MAN;

INCLUDING A COMPREHENSIVE VIEW OF

## CHURCH HISTORY,

AND THE FULFILMENT OF

SCRIPTURE PROPHECIES.

BY THE LATE REVEREND

## JONATHAN EDWARDS,

PRESIDENT OF THE COLLEGE OF NEW JERSEY.

TO WHICH ARE NOW ADDED

## NOTES,

HISTORICAL, CRITICAL, AND THEOLOGICAL,

WITH THE

## LIFE AND EXPERIENCE

OF THE AUTHOR.

*Whoso is wise, and will consider these things, even they shall understand the loving kindness of the* LORD.———Psa. cvii.

NEW-YORK:

Printed by T. and J. Swords, for the Editor,

M,DCC,XCIII.

Edwards's sermon series on the history of the work of redemption, first preached in 1739, went unpublished until after his death. Edited by his son Jonathan Edwards Jr., the series was first published in Edinburgh in 1774. Here is the title page of the first American edition, published in 1793.

He then notes that Christ is the fullness, who fills every-thing in every way (Eph. 2:22–23). In other words, Christ gives meaning and shape to everything and everything is subject to him. Everything finds its center in Christ. This teaching is not restricted to Paul; it fills all of Scripture. Like a great beam ever giving support to a grand structure, Christ and his plan of redemption gird up and sustain the whole text. Edwards continually came across this principle in his reading of the text. One verse in Isaiah, however, par-ticularly managed to catch his attention. He was so capti-vated by this one text that he developed a series of no fewer than thirty sermons on it. Of course, he did not restrict his sermons to this one verse. He used the text much like a gateway pointing the direction to this abundant and mani-fold theme in Scripture.

Edwards chose Isaiah 51:8 as his text. It might be helpful to consider verse 7 as well. This passage reads:

> Hear me, you who know what is right, you people who have my law in your hearts: Do not fear the reproach of men or be terrified by their insults. For the moth will eat them up like a garment; the worm will devour them like wool. But my righteousness will last forever, my salvation through all generations.

Edwards immediately points out the context of this pas-sage:

> The design of this chapter is to comfort the church under her sufferings, and the persecutions of her enemies; and the argument of consolation insisted on is the constancy and perpetuity of God's mercy and faithfulness towards her, which shall be manifest in continuing to work salvation for her, protecting her against all assaults of her enemies, and

carrying her safely through all the changes of the world, and finally crowning her with victory and deliverance.

It is fitting that Edwards uses a text from Isaiah. Writing on the eve of Israel's exile, the prophet anticipates both the coming judgment and deliverance. During the exile itself, however, the promises of deliverance would appear to be quite far off. The destruction of Israel, the Holy City, and the Temple would all give reason for the exiles to question and to wonder about God and his plan for his people. The appearances of things would cause them to be rather desolate and in need of such comfort.

Edwards applies this dynamic to the church throughout the ages, as well as to his own congregation. It is not too much of a stretch to apply it to our time. We know that God is in control and that God is working out his purposes. It's just that sometimes the appearances are to the contrary. God's salvation, his grand scheme of redemption, however, is the reality. And this, Edwards points out, is "to comfort the church."

This comfort centers in God's salvation, his unalterable and eternal plan of redemption. And this salvation stems from God's righteousness. Edwards explains the relationship this way and introduces the covenant of grace into the discussion:

> God's righteousness, or covenant mercy, is the root of which his salvation is the fruit. Both of them relate to the covenant of grace. The one is God's covenant mercy or faithfulness, the other intends that work of God by which this covenant mercy is accomplished in the fruits of it. For salvation is the sum of all those works of God by which the benefits that are by the covenant of grace are procured and bestowed.

Edwards refers to the covenant of grace, or that theological construct which governs the whole of Scripture and first finds expression in the promise of redemption in Genesis 3:15. The promise of the "seed of the woman" finds its fulfillment in Christ. Once again, Paul teaches that "when the time had fully come, God sent his Son, born of a woman, born under law, to redeem those under law, that we might receive the full rights of sons" (Gal. 4:4–5). The covenant of grace further serves to unify Scripture. As Edwards observes:

> The various dispensations of God during this space, belong to the same work, and to the same design, and have all one issue; and therefore are all to be reckoned but as several successive motions of one machine to bring about in the conclusion one great event.

Edwards utilizes this doctrine of the covenant of grace throughout the sermon series. He offers a rather succinct summary of it in the doctrine for the discourse: "The work of redemption is a work that God carries on from the fall of man to the end of the world."

## The Sermon Series

Even though it is a lengthy sermon series, Edwards still follows the typical Puritan sermon format of giving a text, a doctrine, and an application or "improvement." Instead of applying this structure to each sermon, however, he applies the structure to the whole series. Consequently, the first sermon defines the term *redemption* and then develops the "design" or purposes of redemption. Picking up with the next sermon, Edwards puts forth the notion that God's grand plan of redemption has three main periods: (1) from the fall to the incarnation; (2) from the incarnation to the

---

**FIG. 7.3**

**The Work of Redemption:
The Sum of All God's Works**

|  | Period 1 | Period 2 | Period 3 |
|---|---|---|---|
| Begins with | the fall of man | the incarnation of Christ | the resurrection of Christ |
| Ends with | the incarnation of Christ | the resurrection of Christ | the end of the world |

---

resurrection; and (3) from the resurrection to the end of the world.

Edwards's Christocentrism is rather transparent in this division of redemptive history into three periods. The first period concerns the events leading up to the first coming of Christ as it looks forward to Christ. The second period, by only covering thirty-odd years, is rather disproportionate to the centuries and millennia covered in the other two. Nevertheless, Christ's life and his accomplishment of redemption is such a significant period in the unfolding of God's plan that it warrants separate treatment. The final period looks back to Christ's first coming and the work he accomplished. It also looks at the present application of Christ's work in already bringing about redemption. Finally, it looks forward to the second coming of Christ and the consummation of his kingdom. In other words, Edwards's philosophy of history, just like his understanding of Scripture and theology, is radically Christocentric.

These three periods, or "propositions" of the doctrine, also constitute the majority of the sermons. From the second sermon through the twenty-fourth, Edwards exposits God's dealings with both his people and his enemies as his plan for the world unfolds. Edwards leaves virtually no stone unturned as he moves from biblical history to the story of the past two millennia, drawing attention to the ways in which God is bringing his plan to fruition.

He uses the last five sermons to make numerous applications of all this material. He observes that God's plan of redemption offers "great evidence of the truth of the Christian religion," that God's plan teaches the church to endure hardship and suffering, and that it teaches that God will keep his promises. When Edwards finally makes it to the last sermon, he offers a series of detailed applications that mainly cause us to contemplate the character of God in light of his plan for the world.

Below we take a close look at the first and last sermons. In the first sermon, we see Edwards define the term *redemption* and uncover the main things that God is accomplishing through his plan of redemption. In the final sermon, Edwards addresses what may be referred to as the problem of perspective. That is, he confronts the anxiety and fear that arise from not being able to see the end of all things coming together. He gets at this through a discussion of the wonderful doctrine of providence. We will not be looking at the middle of the series, or at the second to the twenty-ninth sermons. But, in these sermons, Edwards joins with a number of other great Christian thinkers and works, such as Augustine and his monumental treatise *The City of God,* in offering a philosophy of history. Along the way he helps us see how all the pieces, both biblical and extra-biblical, fit into the puzzle.

## The Big Picture

Before Edwards starts his hearers and readers on a journey through the history of God's plan of redemption, he wants to explain his terms and show what God designed his great work to accomplish. He wants to make sure that we know what he is talking about and that as he moves us into a close examination of the details we don't lose sight of the big picture.

Edwards is particularly concerned with defining the word *redemption*. He notes that the word may be used in a limited sense, to refer to Christ's work of humiliation on the cross in which he purchased our deliverance from sin and death. "But," Edwards observes, "sometimes the word redemption is taken more largely, including all that God accomplishes tending to this end." This would include all of the works of God in preparation for redemption, the accomplishment of it, and the application of it. And, Edwards adds, "It includes not only what Christ the Mediator has done, but also what the Father and the Holy Spirit have done, as united or confederated in this design of redeeming sinful men." Edwards intends the larger meaning in this discourse as he sees all of these elements conspiring together to form one grand work that spans the ages through eternity.

In addition to understanding the term *redemption*, Edwards wants us to think about the big picture of what God intends to accomplish. Edwards illustrates the need for such a big picture by using the analogy of building a great palace. He observes:

> Suppose an architect, with a great number of hands, were building some great palace; and one that was a stranger to such things should stand by, and see some men digging in the earth, others bringing timber, others hewing stones, and the like. He might see that there was a great deal done; but if he knew not the design, it would all appear to him confusion. And therefore, that the great works and dispensations of God that belong to this great affair of redemption may

not appear like confusion to you, I would set before you briefly the *main things* designed to be accomplished.

Edwards proceeds to list five main things. The first design concerns God's enemies and those that stand contrary to his purpose. Returning to the first promise of Christ and his redemption in Genesis 3:15, we see this conflict between God and his enemies. There will be enmity and strife between the seed of the woman and the seed of the serpent, and Christ will "crush his head," but the serpent will "strike his heel." Consequently, Edwards argues that the first design of redemption "is to put all God's enemies under his feet, and that his goodness may finally appear triumphant over all evil." God designed that his grace will triumph over guilt and that Christ's righteousness will triumph over humanity's sin.

God does not simply triumph over his enemies and cancel out sin's debt, but he "restores all the ruins of the fall" and brings about the "restitution of all things." Here we need to think globally about sin and its effects on redemption and its accomplishment. Not only are we made new creatures, but, according to 2 Peter 3:13, we also look for the new heaven and the new earth. Edwards argues that this work began immediately after the fall and will someday be consummated in the future.

Edwards points out that God also intends "to gather together in one all things in Christ." God is bringing together "all elect creatures, in heaven and in earth, to a union one to another in one body, under one head, and to unite all together in one body to God the father." This theme becomes quite important to Edwards in another sermon series on 1 Corinthians 13 regarding the ethic of love, or Christian charity. In chapter 12 we will see how this theme informs

Edwards's concept of heaven and also how he uses our future activity as a motivation for our ethic in this life.

The fourth design of God's plan of redemption concerns the maturation and perfection of his people. God intended, notes Edwards, "to bring the elect to perfect excellency and beauty in his holy image, which is the proper beauty of spiritual beings, and to advance them to a glorious degree of honour, and raise them to an ineffable height of pleasure and joy." God is fitting us for heaven, so to speak. Edwards will utilize this theme throughout the discourse to remind us of the proper perspective on suffering and apparent setbacks. Far from being an obstacle to God's plan, such events are used by God for the very accomplishing of his purposes.

Finally, Edwards discusses the overarching aim of God's plan of redemption as glorifying "the blessed Trinity in an eminent degree." Edwards sees redemption as God's chosen means to accomplish this end of glorifying himself:

> God had a design of glorifying himself from eternity; yea to glorify each person in the Godhead. The *end* must be considered as first in order of nature, and then the means. And, therefore, we must conceive, that God having confessed his end, had then as it were the means to choose; and the principal means that he adopted was this great work of redemption.

Edwards finds proof for this in the words of Christ recorded in John 13: "Now is the Son of Man glorified and God is glorified in him. If God is glorified in him, God will glorify the Son in himself, and will glorify him at once." (John 13:31–32)

Edwards then notes in the conclusion to the first sermon that this work of redemption divides into three periods as mentioned above. Throughout the series, Edwards stops to apply the doctrine that he is developing to his listeners. He reserves the majority of application, however, to the final few sermons in the series. The last sermon in particular is replete with application of this material, and to this sermon we now turn.

## A Large, Long River

Edwards makes a number of specific points of application in this last sermon. Many of them concern the character of God. He notes that God's plan of redemption reveals his goodness, mercy, faithfulness, wisdom, and above all his glory. He shows the profound implications that the character of God has for living the Christian life in obedience to and dependence on him. He also discusses the implications of the preeminence of Christ over all things. Christ "reigns in uncontrolled power and immense glory," and in the end, he reigns supreme. Knowing the end helps a great deal in the meantime. This perhaps becomes the theme of Edwards's application. This is especially the case in his point of application concerning the doctrine of providence.

Edwards begins this point by noting that God has designed his plan of redemption "to show us the consistency, order, and beauty of God's works of providence." He continues to observe that "if we behold events in any other view, all will look like confusion, like the tossing of waves; things will look as one confused revolution came to pass after another, merely by blind chance, without any regular or certain end." Through the lens of providence, however, we see the events of history and the events of our lives as an orderly series, "all wisely directed in excellent harmony and consistence, tending all to one end." "All God's works of providence," he continues, "meet at last as so many lines meeting in one center."

Just as the multiple aspects of God's work of redemption are unified, so, too, God's providence is but one work. In a rather memorable and vivid illustration, Edwards likens providence to a large and long river that eventually runs its intended course:

> God's providence may not unfitly be compared to a large and long river, having innumerable branches, beginning in different regions, and at a great distance one from another, and all conspiring to one common issue. After their very diverse and apparent contrary courses, they all collect together, the nearer they come to their common end, and at length discharge themselves at one mouth into the same ocean.

Edwards acknowledges, however, that given our limited perspective, we do not always see the end so clearly. In fact, this grand plan is typically lost on one who stands by one of the streams. He continues:

> The different streams of this river are apt to appear like mere confusion to us, because of our limited sight, whereby we cannot see the whole at once. A man who sees but one or two streams at a time, cannot tell what their course tends to. Their course seems very crooked, and different streams seem to run for a while different and contrary ways: and if we view things at a distance, there seem to be innumerable obstacles and impediments in the way, as rocks and mountains, and the like; to hinder their ever uniting and coming to the ocean; but yet if we trace them, they all unite at last, they all come to the same issue, disgorging themselves in one into the same ocean. Not one of all the streams fails.

So he reminds us of the limits of our perspective and the tendency to see only confusion and obstacles. Edwards's own life could be an example. The smallpox inoculation in the early months of 1758 that ended his life might easily be viewed as a mistake, as a thwarting of God's plan for his life. Edwards left so much work behind, including the revising of these sermons, and his life seems tragically cut short. Yet, in God's providence, this was exactly the plan for Edwards's life. Edwards's illustration of providence helps us to take comfort in the reality of God's sovereignty and in his control of all things.

To be sure, Edwards offers a philosophy of history in his *History of the Work of Redemption*. But, he also does a great deal more. He offers a helpful grid through which we can both fit together all of the pieces of Scripture and through which we can construct a cohesive theology. Grasping the big picture of God's plan of redemption helps us to make sense of all the details. Edwards also reminds us that there is a center that gives shape and meaning to life and to the world, that this center holds, and that this center is Christ himself.

Finally, through this text, Edwards offers us not only a vision of the end of all things, but also a vision for the meantime. We know that God is working out all things according to his purpose. We know that his plan is for our good. Consequently, we can be assured that his purpose will be accomplished and in this, all appearances to the contrary, we can rest. As Edwards reminds us, "Not one of all these streams fails."

## Note on the Sources

The first Edinburgh edition of *History of the Work of Redemption* (known as the Erskine edition) appears in Edward Hickman's *The Works of Jonathan Edwards* (1834/1974) 1:532–619. An edition based on a transcription of the original sermon booklets appears in John F. Wilson's *A History of the Work of Redemption* (1989), volume 9 in the Yale edition of *The Works of Jonathan Edwards*. Wilson provides a lengthy introduction, numerous footnotes regarding textual and manuscript issues, and a helpful outline of the discourse. *A Jonathan Edwards Reader* (1995) contains the first sermon of the series on which *History* is based (pp. 124–36).

*8*

# SPIDERS AND RAINBOWS
## The Invisible God in the Visible World

*The heavens declare the glory of God;*
*the skies proclaim the work of his hands.*
*Day after day they pour forth speech;*
*night after night they display knowledge.*
—Psalm 19:1–2

Edwards and his Puritan forebears were people of the book. The Bible served as their lifelong companion, their primary text, and their all-sufficient source for life and godliness. The two most famous books of colonial New England, *The New England Primer* and the *Bay Psalm Book*, well testify to the preeminence of Scripture in their lives and worship. Yet, in reality, they were people of two books, the book of Scripture and the book of nature. The former contains God's special revelation and his written Word. The latter contains God's general revelation and, as the Psalmist notes, a language without words. The Puritans indeed devoured the Bible and just as intently and inquisitively pored over the book of nature.

## Reading the Book of Nature

Of course, the Puritans had a proper perspective on the relationship between the two, viewing the book of nature as subordinate to the Bible. Following John Calvin's lead, they held that they could read nature accurately only through the glasses of Scripture. Without the aid of Scripture and without the knowledge of God as both Redeemer and Creator, humanity quickly distorts the revelation of God in this world. Paul vividly portrays this distortion in the opening verses of Romans 1. In the worst deal of all time, the truth was exchanged for a lie, and humanity continues to reap the benefit of perverting the testimony that God has graciously left of himself stamped on his creation and creatures.

But, once the vision is restored through God's work of regeneration, then nature can be seen as the witness to God, declaring his glory, revealing his character, and testifying to his goodness. Edwards's own conversion as related in the "Personal Narrative" bears this out. You might recall from the earlier chapters that Edwards describes his conversion as an altering of appearances, as a new vision of the world. He writes:

> The appearance of everything was altered: there seemed to be as it were a calm, sweet cast, or appearance of divine glory, in almost everything. God's excellency, his wisdom, his purity and love, seemed to appear in everything; in the sun, moon, and stars; in the clouds, and blue sky; in the grass, flowers, trees; in the water, and all nature: which used greatly to fix my mind.

Edwards proceeds to explain how he used to be terrified by thunder, but now he hears "the majestic and awful voice of God's thunder" that leads him "to sweet contemplations of my great and glorious God." Through the Spirit's work of regeneration, Edwards was able to see general revelation and read the book of nature accurately. And he became an avid reader of it.

In addition to Edwards as pastor, theologian, and philosopher, there exists another dimension to the thought and writings of Edwards, that of the scientist. This is not to suggest that these dimensions represented competing or conflicting vocations. Rather, Edwards was able to weave all of these interests together in his lifelong quest of glorifying and enjoying God. His forays into science are found in a number of manuscripts and some finished essays. This current chapter, consequently, is different from the others. They are primarily devoted to a single text. In this one we examine a number of shorter writings as we watch Edwards explore everything from spiders to the vast universe itself. Through these writings Edwards reveals the reality of the invisible God through his visible world.

## Edwards as Scientist

Tradition finds Edwards as a mere twelve-year-old trying his hand at writing for the established scientific community in England. This was based largely on a guess by Sereno E. Dwight. Dwight came across a draft of a "letter" that was really an essay addressed to Judge Paul Dudley, a friend of Edwards's father and a Fellow of the Royal Society of London. This undated manuscript was only a draft. The final copy, although assumed to exist, lay unnoticed, buried among the papers of the New-York Historical Society until George S. Claghorn, compiler of Edwards's letters and personal writings, discovered the final copy sent to Judge Dudley dated October 31, 1723. Edwards was still young at nineteen when he wrote this, but he was not the twelve-year-old prodigy that Dwight had created.

Edwards's nineteenth year found him exploring his options for his life's direction. He had just received his M.A. from Yale the previous month and was currently offering pulpit supply to the church in Bolton, Connecticut. The next year he would return to Yale for a two-year term as tutor before starting his tenure at Northampton. In the fall of 1723, however, all of this was not so clear and Edwards perhaps considered science as his field.

Timothy Edwards encouraged his son to write an essay for his friend Paul Dudley. In one of Dudley's own essays concerning "remarkable instances of the power and nature of vegetation" in New England, he records Timothy's account of a rather notable pumpkin vine. The story was published in the *Philosophical Transactions* of the Royal Society of London. Below follows the account:

> In the year 1669, a single pumpkin seed was accidentally dropp'd in a small pasture where cattle had been fodder'd for some time. This single seed took root of itself, and without any manner of care or cultivation; the vine run along over several fences, and spread over a large piece of ground far and wide, and continued its progress until the frost came and kill'd it. This seed had no more than one stalk, but a very large one, for it measured eight inches round; from this single vine, they gathered two hundred and sixty pumpkins; and, one with another, as big as an half peck; enough to fill a large tumbrel, besides a considerable number of small and unripe pumpkins, that they made no account of.

Timothy's son, following his father's urging, recorded his own observations. Instead of a remarkable pumpkin vine, however, the younger Edwards decided to observe and record the activity of the flying spider. He wrote up those observations in an essay for Paul Dudley. In the introduction to the letter, Edwards notes:

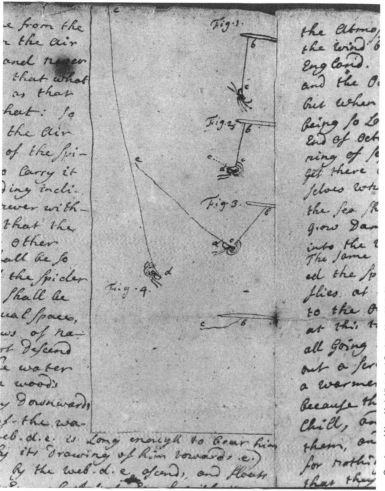

In a letter to Judge Paul Dudley, Edwards provided his own illustration of the flying spider and its movements.

In the postscript of your letter to my father you manifest a willingness that he has observed in nature worthy of remark; that which is the subject of the following lines is thought to be such: he has laid upon me to write the account, I having had advantage to make more full observations. If you think, Sir, that they are not worthy the taking notice of, with greatness and goodness overlook and conceal. They are some things that I have happily seen of the wondrous and curious works of the spider. Although everything pertaining to this insect is admirable, yet there are some phenomena relating to them more particularly wonderful.

Although not all will likely agree with Edwards's assessment that everything about the flying spider is "admirable," his enthusiasm and his probing mind and eye are apparent. One can easily picture Edwards "happily" observing this spider in order to understand why it behaves as it does and in order to appreciate the wisdom and beauty of God's creations—even the insects. The mystery that he attempts to uncover in these observations concerns the apparent "flying" of this particular spider. He writes that "everyone that is used to the country knows of their marching in the air from one tree to another, sometimes at the distance of five or six rods, though they are wholly destitute of wings." He adds that these spiders travel in the air "in a very unaccountable manner." So he sets out to account for it.

Edwards had seen the flying spider on many occasions. Once on a walk through the woods he came across one and here is his account:

> I happened to see one of these spiders on a bush. So I went to the bush and shook it, hoping thereby to make him uneasy upon it and to provoke him to leave it by flying, and took good care that he should not get off from it in any other way. So I continued constantly to shake it . . . till at last the spider was pleased, however, to leave that bush and march along the air to the next; but which way I did not know, nor could I conceive, but resolved to watch him more narrowly the next time.

The next opportunity came and Edwards determined to figure out exactly how this spider "flies." After some more

164

observations and experiments he discovered the answer. The spiders let themselves hang down a little by a web "and then put out a [different] web at their tails, which being so exceeding rare when it first comes from the spider as to be lighter than air, so as of itself it will ascend." He continues to note that the wind takes this web and carries it to great lengths until it attaches to a tree branch or another bush. In this way the spider appears to fly when in reality it is swinging from web to web at great distances. He further explains how the spider moves by freeing itself from the original web and using the new web it just released. So he continues:

> As when a man is at the bottom of the water, if he has hold of a piece of timber so great that the wood's tendency upwards is greater than the man's tendency downwards, he together with the wood will ascend to the surface of the water. Therefore, when the spider perceives that the [new] web is long enough to bear him up by its ascending force . . . he lets go of his hold of the [old] web, ascends and floats in the air with the [new web].

Once you know how spiders move, Edwards notes how easy it is to see them: "Their way of moving may very distinctly be seen if they are held up in the sun, in a calm day, against a dark door or anything that is black." One can just imagine Edwards in the fields around the Connecticut River Valley spending hours carrying around a large piece of wood or cloth and watching the spiders fly through the air on their webs. He also drew a diagram to accompany these observations.

From this discovery, Edwards draws two conclusions. First, he sees the "wisdom of the Creator in providing of the spider" the means to produce the web and to move in this way. He also sees "the exuberant goodness of the Creator, who hath not only provided for all the necessities, but also for the pleasure and recreation of all sorts of creatures, even the insects." Yet, Edwards observes that this process not only serves the flying spider for recreation, but also leads to its destruction. At the end of summer and as the New England breeze turns easterly toward the sea, the spiders are swept into the sea. But here, too, Edwards is convinced of the wisdom of God "that is exercised about such little things in this wonderful contrivance of annually carrying off and burying" these spiders in the ocean floor so that they do not become an overwhelming pestilence.

God's wisdom and care is further seen in that these spiders lay their eggs before they expire. Consequently, "adjusting their destruction to their multiplication," they do not decrease or increase, but remain in equal numbers. Edwards concludes that, while spiders are often considered the "most despicable of animals," from their "glistening webs so much of the wisdom of the Creator shines."

## The Heavens Declare . . .

Edwards moves from insects to the vast sky in his quest to see the handiwork of God in the visible world. Edwards's fascination with the sky, as well as with rainbows, light rays, and even the human eye, owes much to the writings and thought of Isaac Newton. Deists looked at Newton's work and developed the idea of the mechanical world: the world is a finely tuned clock that God wound up and that now runs with perfect precision. This compromises a number of significant doctrines. First, it prohibits the intervention of God in this world and thereby disallows miracles. Second, it vitiates the doctrine of providence, as it argues that God is not actively sustaining his world.

Deists could not admit either of these two doctrines because both point, in their thinking, to a less than perfect world that requires God's intervention to keep it running correctly, like an imperfect watch that constantly needs to be adjusted and rewound. They thought they were exalting God by restricting his involvement in the world. In reality, they undermined God by limiting his presence in this world.

Edwards looks at Newton and reaches entirely different conclusions. Edwards, like Newton himself, sees God at work through his meticulous and orderly world. The wonders of the visible world attest to God's handiwork as both Creator and Sustainer. This is the case from the smallest— and even most despicable—creatures, like the spider, to the grandest elements, like the stars and the universe itself. Intent on not merely reading Newton, but on applying Newtonian physics in his own observations, Edwards set out to explore the natural phenomena. Two things in particular captured Edwards's gaze: rainbows and light rays. These studies grew out of his coursework for his master's degree at Yale.

Before Edwards looks to the sky, he first is intrigued by the eye itself. He notes, "One thing very evidential of the wisdom of God in the contrivance of the eye, is that it should so easily, perfectly, and distinctly perceive the stroke or the impression of the rays of light, that is many thousands times too weak to be perceived by any other part of the body, besides the retina at the bottom of the eye." We find the eye even more wonderful "if we consider how small the retina of the eye is." The mystery of the anatomy of the eye and our sense of sight amaze Edwards. Even though today we may be better able to explain the anatomy of the eye and while we have made advances in treating it, we can still join with Edwards in amazement of God's handiwork.

Edwards is also concerned with what his eye perceives, light rays and rainbows. Edwards seeks to explain the phe-

nomenon of rainbows by appealing to Newton's understanding of the reflexibility and refrangibility or refraction
of light. Consequently, Edwards attributes rainbows to the
refraction of sunlight in the fine droplets of rain or mist in
the atmosphere, which produces the spectrum of colors. He
also applies Newton's thought to better understand light
rays in general. He offers various calculations of both the
time and distance that light rays pass and of how infinitesi-
mal the rays are when they finally reach the eye.

In fact, Edwards exclaims that when the rays travel the
millions of miles through space, "this will make the rays of
light less than any man will have the patience to make figures for." Consequently, he concludes that the nature of
light rays evidences "the exquisite skill of the artificer whose
fingers have formed these infinitely small bodies." And,
again, he contemplates the skill of God in creating the eye
in such a way that it perceives these rays.

Edwards, as he did with his observations on the spider,
also illustrates these observations through a diagram using
the compass that he requested of his father during his student days in a letter mentioned in chapter 1. In this letter,
dated July 24, 1719, Edwards updates his father on his studies and then makes his request:

> I have inquired of Mr. Cutler what books we should have
> need of the next year. He answered he would have me get
> against that time Alsted's *Geometry* and Gassendi's *Astron-
> omy;* with which I would entreat you to get a pair of dividers,
> or mathematician's compasses, and a scale, which are ab-
> solutely necessary in order to learning mathematics.

While Edwards did not commit his life to the pursuit of
science, he nevertheless realized the value of the endeavor.
He continued his observations and his contemplations

throughout his life. Edwards's two main activities for exercise were chopping wood and riding horseback. As he rode through the Connecticut River Valley, he probably thought about the sermon he would preach on the next Sabbath, and the next page of the book he was writing. And more than likely, he also thought about those spiders he had observed so many times flying through the air.

Edwards agreed with the hymn writer that this is in fact "my Father's world." As he explored the behavior of spiders, the nature of light rays, and the mechanics of the eye, he applied the same intensity that he expended on his studies of theology and the Bible, so he could better understand God and his work in this world.

## Stunned by Beauty

Beauty is probably more easily identified than defined. Nevertheless, Edwards takes a stab at defining it by turning to the conceptions of harmony and excellency put forth by Plato. Edwards expresses these concepts by referring to the sweet mutual consents of this world with itself and to its maker. The beauty of the physical world far outdistances any work of art that humans can produce. It is also a mere shadow of the invisible and spiritual beauty that it represents.

Edwards readily admits the mysterious dynamic and nature of how the beauty of the world captivates us. He also admits the difficulty in explaining the harmony and excellency that define beauty. "Thus we find ourselves pleased in beholding the color of the violets," he observes, "but we know not what secret regularity or harmony it is that creates that pleasure in our minds." Nevertheless, he stands in awe of the beauty of God's creation.

Edwards also finds this beauty in the world to offer meaning and to engender a zest for life, even in the face of pain and misery. In his brief essay on the beauty of the world, he concludes that the world's harmony and beauty are

> the reason why almost all men, and those that seem to be very miserable, love life: because they cannot bear to lose the sight of such a beautiful and lovely world—the ideas, that every moment while we live have a beauty that we take not distinct notice of, but bring a pleasure that, when we come to trial, we had rather live in much pain and misery than lose.

Edwards further discovers this world to be a testimony to God's care for his creatures. Specifically, he sees God as "preserver, benevolent benefactor, and fountain of all happiness." God not only created this world, but also actively sustains and upholds it. Further, God abundantly provides for his creation and creatures through his omnibenevolence. Turning to the original creation account, Edwards notes that, according to Genesis, when God had finished his work, he "saw all that he had made, and it was very good" (Gen. 1:31).

God's work in creation also testifies that he is the "fountain of all happiness." Contained in the creation account is a short phrase that often gets overlooked. Concerning the creation of trees, Genesis 2 indicates that these objects have a twofold purpose: to be both "pleasing to the eye and good for food." There is the purpose of utility as the earth provides sustenance for us. But there is also an aesthetic purpose, as this creation is "pleasing to the eye." God's creation is a source of pleasure, recreation, and happiness for his creatures. But, as we mentioned in the beginning of this chapter, Romans 1 reminds us that not everyone sees the world this way.

In fact, there are basically three ways that we can view the world. First, we can regard the world as chaos and confusion. This is a rather bleak proposal with a grim outcome. Second, we can regard the world as orderly, but view this order rather mechanically and account for it in purely naturalistic terms. One thinks of Carl Sagan's dictum, "The Cosmos is all there ever was, all there is, and all there ever will be." Although not as bleak as the first proposal, this view still leaves a great number of questions about the origin and purpose of the world unanswered. In other words, it fails to answer the ultimate question: Why? Finally, we can see the world as orderly, purposeful, and meaningful. And we account for this by looking to a Creator. The world *is*, and it is meaningful because it is created by God for his purpose and glory.

Edwards reminds us that this is the only coherent way to view the world. And he also reminds us, especially in our increasingly technological age, to take the time to contemplate our surroundings, to explore the mysteries of the natural world, and to see the stamp of the Creator's wisdom, beauty, and goodness on his entire creation. Through these writings, Edwards helps us to see the invisible God in the visible world.

## Note on the Sources

The essays and short writings referred to in this chapter may be found in Wallace E. Anderson's *Scientific and Philosophical Writings* (1980), volume 6 of the Yale edition of *The Works of Jonathan Edwards*. The following essays were cited: "Of Insects" (pp. 154–62), "The Spider Letter" (pp. 163–69), "Of the Rainbow" (pp. 298–301), "Of Light Rays" (pp. 302–304), "Beauty of the World" (pp. 305–306), and "The Wisdom of God in the Contrivance of the World" (pp. 307–310). Anderson's introduction (pp. 1–143) gives great detail of the development of Edwards's scientific and philosophical thought. "The Spider Letter" and "The Beauty of the World" are also available in *A Jonathan Edwards Reader* (1995), pages 1–8 and 14–15.

# 9

# UNDERSTANDING THE WILL

*Freedom of the Will*

*This book alone is sufficient to establish its author as the greatest philosopher-theologian yet to grace the American scene.*

—Paul Ramsey

*It is the glory and greatness of the Divine Sovereign, that his will is determined by his own infinite, all-sufficient wisdom in everything.*

—Jonathan Edwards,
*Freedom of the Will*

One of the most confusing, contested, and heated issues today concerns human freedom and responsibility, on the one hand, and the sovereignty of God and his decrees, on the other. If you want to start a long conversation with just about anyone, then simply take a stand on this issue. The truth is, however, that this is not a new problem. From its inception, the church has endeavored to untie this Gordian knot. As you survey the great thinkers and works that have taken up this challenge, among them stand Augustine's work in both the *City of God* and *The Freedom of the Will,* Martin Luther's magisterial *The Bondage of the Will* (a work, by the way, which Luther viewed as getting at the very heart of Reformation theology), and book 2 of John Calvin's *The Institutes of the Christian Religion.* And clearly Jonathan Edwards's *Freedom of the Will* takes its stand among them as well.

This work has been considered Edwards's greatest literary achievement and, according to many, ranks him as one of America's greatest theologians and philosophers. When it first came out in 1754, it captivated readers on both sides of the Atlantic and it continues to gratify readers to this day.

Edwards had begun his research and thinking about the book as early as 1746. In a letter to Joseph Bellamy in January of that year, he notes, "I have been reading Whitby, which has engaged me pretty thoroughly in the study of the Arminian controversy; and I have written considerably upon it in my private papers." Two years later he informs Bellamy that he is still "engaged in studies on the Arminian controversy and preparing to write something upon them." By 1752 his research was almost concluded, and in a letter to John Erskine he sketches the outline of his forthcoming book. We next find Edwards mentioning the book in 1753, when he lets his friends know that it will soon be available, and again in 1754. In the spring of this year, in a letter to Thomas Foxcroft, he expresses his impatience with the printer as he awaits the publication of his treatise.

In fairness to his publisher, some of the delay had to do with Edwards's almost constant revision of fine points of the text. But in 1754 Samuel Kneeland, Edwards's Boston publisher, succeeded in getting Edwards's manuscript pages through the press and into the many hands anxious to have Edwards's thoughts on the "Arminian controversy."

## The Arminian Controversy

From the time that Edwards preached the Boston lecture sermon, "God Glorified in the Work of Redemption," in 1731, he was considered to be a formidable defender of the Augustinian and Calvinistic understanding of the will. This view dominated Puritan thought, writings, and sermons in both Old and New England. In the beginning decades of the eighteenth century, however, the cohesion of this doctrine among the Puritans began to crack and to show the potential of coming undone.

The term *Arminianism* derives from Jacobus Arminius (1560–1609), a Dutch theologian who originally advocated Calvinism but began to question the Calvinist view of predestination and the atonement. His followers expressed their view in the *Remonstrance* (1610), which emphasizes human response and free will in salvation. The *Remonstrance* consisted of five points and was challenged by the Canons of the Synod of Dort (1618). At Dort, a group of Calvinist theologians responded to each of the five points of the *Remonstrance,* which are summarized in the popular acrostic TULIP as a summary of Calvinist teaching.

Some prominent clergy, such as Boston's Charles Chauncey and Harvard President John Leverett, advocated Arminian principles and influenced the Congregational churches of New England. On the other side of the Atlantic, three authors in particular furthered the Arminian controversy: Thomas Chubb, Daniel Whitby, and the hymn writer Isaac Watts.

Watts, it may be recalled, played a major role in seeing Edwards's *Faithful Narrative* come to the press. On this issue, however, Watts found himself criticized by Edwards for advocating a more moderate form of Calvinism, although he was far closer to Edwards and the Calvinist position than were Chubb and Whitby. In fact, Edwards reluctantly criticizes Watts, not referring to him by name and also couching his criticism with comments of deep respect.

Both Chubb and Whitby published detailed defenses of the Arminian position, and Whitby's work in particular appears again and again throughout the pages of Edwards's *Freedom of the Will.* These works by Chubb and Whitby presented impressive challenges to the deeply ingrained beliefs of Puritanism, and they demanded an answer. Edwards took up the challenge.

Throughout his ministry, as we have seen on numerous occasions, Edwards found himself embroiled in controversy. Again, his attitude here models a healthy approach to dealing with conflict. In the preface to the work, Edwards explains his motives and method in writing this book. He notes that he hesitated to use the label "Arminian," as he did not want "to stigmatize persons of any sort with a name of reproach." He continues, however, to point out the difficulties of the alternative designation of "these men" as bad manners. He also points out that while he claims the title "Calvinist," he does not hold to the tenets of Calvinism just because Calvin held and taught them. Given his demeanor, he probably would have preferred to avoid this controversy, as well as the others in his life. Nevertheless, he thought the issue to be of grave importance. He ends his preface addressing the urgency of the issue:

> The subject is of such importance, as to *demand* attention, and the most thorough consideration. Of all kinds of knowledge that we can ever obtain, the knowledge of God and the knowledge of ourselves are the most important. . . . The knowledge of ourselves consists chiefly in right apprehensions concerning those two chief faculties of our nature, the *understanding* and *will.* Both are very important: yet the science of the latter must be confessed to be of greatest mo-

ment; inasmuch as all virtue and religion have their seat more immediately in the will. . . . And the grand question about the Freedom of the Will, is the main point that belongs to the science of the Will. Therefore, I say, the importance of the subject greatly *demands* the attention of Christians.

In other words, if we follow Edwards's chain of reasoning, the issue of the freedom of the will is the central question regarding the nature and exercise of the human will. And the will is at the very center of a proper knowledge of humanity, God, and religion, or humanity's relationship to God. Consequently, he engaged the Arminian controversy not necessarily to defend Calvinism, but because he thought these issues to be central "to the great business for which we were created," the business of religion and the relationship that we have with God.

After the preface, Edwards proceeds to divide his work into four parts and a conclusion. In part 1 he defines his terms and explains the issues involved. His attention primarily focuses on *necessity, ability,* and *agency.* These terms get at the heart of the will, and a proper understanding of them enables one to understand the final term he explains, *liberty.* In part 2, he considers the Arminian position and whether or not the Arminian view of freedom can be sustained. Along the way he points out some inconsistencies of the view and considers the challenges that God's foreknowledge and decrees present to the Arminian conception of freedom.

Part 3 contains an extensive treatment of one objection to the Calvinist view, the question of responsibility and judgment in light of the bondage of the will. Edwards tackles this problem by first showing how the Arminian view, which demands freedom in order for there to be responsibility and fairness in judgment, is not without its own problems. Finally, Edwards raises a series of objections in part 4. He also answers these objections and shows the Calvinist position to be scriptural, rational, and consistent. He ends the treatise with a brief conclusion outlining the implications of one's position on the will. Here he expands beyond the narrow question of the will and touches on issues related to the infamous TULIP.

Like some other works we have examined, the nature of *A Careful and Strict Enquiry into the Modern Prevailing Notions of that Freedom of Will which Is Supposed To Be Essential to Moral Agency, Virtue and Vice, Reward and Punishment, Praise and Blame* is such that we can only hit some of the highlights. Below we will explore Edwards's main point or thesis and point to a few other crucial teachings from this text. It is impossible to do full justice to this work in this brief chapter, but hopefully we will whet the appetite for further study of this skillful treatment of an important subject.

## Moral Inability

The shorter version of Edwards's title, *Freedom of the Will,* may be a little misleading. Luther's title of his own work on the subject, *The Bondage of the Will,* seems more accurate in representing the position. Edwards, to be sure, comes down on the same side as Luther. He does present the issue, however, in a rather intriguing and thought-provoking way by addressing the nature of both freedom and the will. Let's first look at the will.

Early in his definition of the will, Edwards argues that something drives the will or causes it to choose one thing over another. The will, he concludes, is determined. This, of course, raises the question of what determines it. He offers a preliminary answer by observing, "It is that motive, which, as it stands in the view of the mind, is the strongest that determines the will." This ground motive underlies the will and directs it. Perhaps this motive may be understood as the chief essence of our nature, or our defining characteristic. Edwards refers to it simply as our nature. It is what makes us who we are. Edwards further reasons that the will acts in agreement with this motive. We could put the matter this way: the will chooses what the will wants, and this motive behind the will, or our nature, determines what the will wants.

Edwards's next move is to associate this line of thought with what he refers to as "moral inability." He defines this concept when he writes, "moral inability consists in the opposition or want [lack] of inclination." This lack of inclination may also be due to contrary inclinations. We can see Edwards's point more clearly when we apply it to the problem of sin. At the fall of Adam, humanity not only fell out of favor with God, but also lost the ability to please God or achieve righteousness. Consequently, one depends on the righteousness of Christ and his ability to reconcile us to God. Without Christ, humanity is in a state of moral inability.

This moral inability, or what Paul refers to as the sin nature, governs the will. In this sense the will acts according to its determination; it chooses and acts upon the nature that underlies it. In this sense the will is free, but only so far as it acts according to its own nature. Edwards concedes that we have the natural ability to will and then to do many things, but because of sin, we have moral inability and this moral inability governs the will. He next addresses the problem of defining freedom.

## Understanding Freedom

If we think a little further about Edwards's understanding of the will, we can see that Edwards preserves the integrity of the will. We can also see how one can then speak of freedom or consider his or her actions to be free. But, again, this freedom extends to a consistency with one's nature. This leads Edwards to discuss the nature of liberty or freedom. He notes that the Arminian notion of freedom entails self-determining power and contingency. Both of these need explaining, and he spends a great amount of time in part 2 developing them. We can briefly summarize these two concepts.

By "self-determining power" Edwards means "a certain sovereignty the will has over itself, and its own acts, whereby it determines its own volitions; so as not to be dependent, in its determinations, on any cause without itself, nor determined to anything prior to its own acts." By contingency he intends that which is "opposed to all necessity, or any fixed and certain connection with some previous ground or reason of its existence." These two then provide the "essence of liberty," according to the Arminian, and, without them, humanity "has no real freedom." This understanding of freedom underlies the Arminian concept of moral agency and responsibility. Only moral agents who are truly and absolutely free, goes the argument, can be held responsible for their actions.

Edwards considered this position to give too little credence to the effect of sin upon the will and to miss the true meaning of freedom, although he recognizes the problem of accounting for human responsibility. Further, if freedom means the contingency of things upon an undetermined choice, then Edwards also sees problems in reconciling this view with the doctrine of God's sovereignty and decrees. But what if freedom had to do with something other than choice and self-determining power?

Edwards answers this question by asking yet another: When will humanity be most free? He answers that this will be in heaven in the glorified state. He also ponders the question, What being has the most freedom? and answers that it is God. In both ideas he finds an answer to the Arminian view and the true meaning of freedom. In both cases freedom has little to do with self-determining power and contingency. Rather, freedom has to do with acting according to one's nature.

Once again, the fall of Adam helps us understand this concept. Humanity was created to worship, serve, and have fellowship with God. Yet, all of this is hindered due to the fall. Consequently, Paul speaks of humanity as being bound to sin. Paul likes to refer to us prior to salvation as slaves to sin and to our conversion as redemption, or as purchase from the enslavement of sin. In other words, salvation restores us to our intended role and enables us to do what we were created to do and to be what we were created to be. In heaven, in our glorified state and entirely without our sinful nature, we will fully be who we were intended to be, even though we will not be able to choose to sin or not sin. Consequently, Edwards argues that freedom has little to do with choice in the sense of self-determining power and contingency.

If we think about this in terms of God, then we can see how he is the being with the most freedom. He is absolutely free and does not need to come into being through making choices, as he is perfect. Edwards explains it this way: "The glorified saints have not their freedom at all diminished, in any respect; and . . . God himself has the highest possible freedom, according to the true and proper meaning of the term."

Edwards still has to contend with the issue of moral agency. If freedom does not have to do with self-determining power and contingency, then Edwards argues that moral agency does not require these things either. To be a moral agent, according to Edwards, instead requires "a being that is capable of those actions that have a moral quality, and which can properly be denominated good or evil in a moral sense," and a being with "a sense of moral good and evil, or of such a thing as desert or worthiness, of praise or blame, reward or punishments."

Edwards also illustrates this by viewing God as a moral agent. After Edwards considers God to be the most free, he also considers him to be the highest example of moral agency. In the process, he contrasts necessity with contingency. Contingency involves a choice and options; necessity does not. Consequently, moral agency is not based on contingency. He writes:

> God is in the highest possible respect, an agent, and active in the exercise of his infinite holiness; though he acts therein in the highest degree, necessarily; and his actions of this kind are in the highest, most absolutely perfect, manner virtuous and praiseworthy; and are so, for that very reason, because they are most perfectly necessary.

God is necessarily holy and his will is determined to that which is good. Absent from God is contingency or choice in this sense. Yet, we are commanded to ascribe virtue to God, and, of course, he acts in an entirely praiseworthy way.

Edwards continues to deal with the objection that true responsibility demands freedom defined by choice throughout the treatise. At one point he quotes Daniel Whitby, voicing this objection rather directly. Whitby states, "If all human actions are necessary, virtue and vice must be empty names; we being capable of nothing that is blameworthy, or deserveth praise; for who could blame a person for doing what he could not help, or judge that he deserveth praise only for what he could not avoid?" In other words, how can you blame a sinner for sinning?

This objection represents perhaps the perennial stumbling block to the doctrine of predestination and a heavy view of the sovereignty of God. It is not unlike the challenge to God's sovereign election that Paul refers to in his analogy of the potter and the clay in Romans 9. Paul asks rhetorically, "Shall what is formed say to him who formed it, 'Why did you make me like this?'" (Rom. 9:20). Paul answers by noting the potter's exclusive right over the pottery.

Edwards essentially devotes all of part 3 to answering this question. He starts by reiterating the point above concerning God's virtue in light of his necessary and not contingent moral excellency. He also looks to the incarnation and sees virtue in the acts of Christ during his life on earth. Edwards further turns to specific accounts in Scripture, such as Romans 1:28, where God gives sinful humanity over to a depraved mind, and the account about Judas. This objection, in effect, becomes an objection against Scripture.

## According to His Will

In part 4 Edwards offers the final answer to the Arminian notion of free will by stressing that God's will determines all things. As Edwards declares, "The sovereignty of God is his ability and authority to do whatever pleases him." He explores the rich contours of the sovereignty of God by looking at the different elements related to it. He observes that the sovereignty is exercised according to

supreme, universal, and infinite *power;* whereby he is able to do what he pleases, without any control, without any confinement of that power, without any subjection, in the least measure, to any other power; and so without any hindrance or restraint, that it should be either impossible, or at all difficult for him to accomplish his will.

God also has supreme authority and the "absolute and most perfect right to do what he wills," as he is the "head of all dominion and fountain of all authority." God is not at all subject to the wills of others; instead all other wills are "perfectly subject to his." Finally, Edwards sees God's sovereign will as governed by God's own wisdom. Edwards quotes Isaiah 40:14: "Whom did the LORD consult to enlighten him, and who taught him the right way? Who was it that taught him knowledge or showed him the path of understanding?" So Edwards writes that God's wisdom is "supreme, perfect, underived, self-sufficient, and independent." Having explored these contours to God's sovereignty, he concludes:

> There is no other divine sovereignty but this; and this is properly *absolute sovereignty*. No other is desirable; nor would any other be honourable, or happy, and indeed, there is no other conceivable or possible. It is the glory and greatness of the Divine Sovereign, that his will is determined by his own infinite, all-sufficient wisdom in everything.

Edwards adds that God's will brings about what God determines to be "the fittest and best" for his creatures. It only follows that if God's will is governed by his wisdom, then that which is determined is "most wise." And, if God is perfectly able to accomplish his will, then we can be sure that his will will be accomplished and we can know that he is working all things for good. In a memorable line, Edwards notes that "God does not do what he does, or order what he orders, accidentally or unawares." Instead, like a grand conductor, God orchestrates and brings to pass all things according to his will.

## All the Glory to God and Christ

After Edwards had completed *Freedom of the Will,* he was far from finished with the Arminian controversy. His name continued to come up in the writings of others, and he continued to think about the issues. In a letter to his friend John Erskine, dated August 3, 1757, shortly before he left Stockbridge, Edwards offers perhaps his clearest and most succinct thoughts on the issue of the freedom of the will. In this letter he reiterates many key concepts from *Freedom of the Will* and explores the implications of the issue for pastoral ministry and one's relationship to God.

Edwards begins by explaining that the notion of liberty, "consisting in a contingent self-determination of the will, as necessary to the morality of men's dispositions and actions," is "inconceivably pernicious." The opposite view of freedom, as understood as related to necessity, by contrast is "one of the most important truths of moral philosophy that ever was discussed and most necessary to be known." Edwards finds this most important truth to be at the very heart of helping one to see his or her true need of Christ. "A bad will, or an evil disposition of heart," is the essence of one's sin and the sum of one's wickedness.

A bad will is also the key to seeing our inability to merit salvation or God's favor. Ignoring this and emphasizing humanity's ability to choose God prevents people from being "brought off from all their dependence on their own righteousness." In fact, "things of this kind have visibly been the main hindrance of the true humiliation and conversion of sinners, in the times of awakening, that have been in this land."

A scenario in which the sinner chooses Christ also diminishes the nature of true faith, as "man is not dependent on God; but God is rather dependent on man in this affair;

for he only acts consequentially, in acts in which he depends on what he sees we determine and do first." Edwards then contrasts this with faith: "The nature of true faith implies a disposition to give all the glory of our salvation to God and Christ." In *Freedom of the Will,* he explains this truth this way: "The conversion of a sinner [is] not owing to a man's self-determination, but to God's determination, and eternal election, which is absolute, and depending on the sovereign will of God, and not on the free will of man." Consequently, Edwards puts forth a view of the will, freedom, and salvation that reserves all of the glory for God.

This comprises Edwards's contribution to this all-important issue. He reminds us that there is something that drives the choices we make, which in turn result in the thoughts and actions that comprise our lives; behind our will lies our true nature. He reminds us that we cannot ignore the problem of sin and downplay sin's effects on the will. When we talk about the freedom of the will, Edwards also reminds us that we have to be clear in our conceptions of both the will and freedom. Too often, we think of freedom as demanding choice. Instead, he reminds us that freedom is better viewed as acting in consistency with our nature.

Outside of Christ, we are free. Unfortunately, that freedom is exercised toward and bound by sin. We are oriented away from God and falsely content with ourselves. In Christ, we are also free. But, we are free indeed. That is, we are free to do what God created us to do. And we are free to be what God intends us to be.

## Note on the Sources

*Freedom of the Will* is available in the Hickman edition of *The Works of Jonathan Edwards* (1834/1974), 1:1–93; and in Paul Ramsey's *The Freedom of the Will* (1957), volume 1 of theYale edition of *The Works of Jonathan Edwards.* Selections from the book appear in most anthologies of Edwards's writings, including *A Jonathan Edwards Reader* (1995), pages 192–222. The letters referred to in this chapter may all be found in George S. Claghorn's *Letters and Personal Writings* (1998), volume 16 in the Yale edition of *The Works of Jonathan Edwards.*

PART 4

## SERMONS

Edwards was foremost a pastor, and his primary genre was the sermon. He left behind approximately 1,400 sermons, some very well known and others barely studied. In part 4 we examine only three of them. The first is perhaps the most famous of all American sermons, "Sinners in the Hands of an Angry God." Next follows a little-known but insightful and challenging sermon on prayer, "The Most High, a Prayer-Hearing God." Finally, this section ends with a rather different image than the one with which Puritans are typically identified. In the final sermon in *Charity and Its Fruits,* "Heaven Is a World of Love," Edwards explores the glories of heaven.

# 10

# A DOOR OF MERCY

### "Sinners in the Hands of an Angry God"

*I dare the World therefore to show*
*A God like me, to anger slow:*
*Whose Wrath is full of Grace.*
*Doth hate all Sins both Greate, and small:*
*Yet when Repented, pardons all.*
*Frowns with a Smiling Face.*

—Edward Taylor,
*God's Determinations*

*Christ has flung the door of mercy wide open, and stands*
*in the door calling and crying with a loud voice to poor*
*sinners.*

—Jonathan Edwards,
"Sinners in the Hands of
an Angry God"

Enfield, Connecticut, was a long horseback ride straight down the Connecticut River from Northampton. Edwards had traveled this route many times. Only now, as he rode up and down the river, he could see the amazing work of God throughout these Connecticut River Valley towns. In March 1741 Edwards informed a friend, "This winter has been a time of the most remarkable blessing of heaven upon my family that ever was." He continues to note that God is also working in his Northampton congregation and other towns such as Deerfield and Suffield. In fact, in another letter, a few months later, Edwards writes, "Neither earth or hell can hinder this work that is going on in the country. . . . By what I can understand, the work of God is greater at this day in the land, than it has been at any time." But the revival that was spreading up and down the river and throughout New England had yet to reach Enfield.

Edwards had come to Enfield with his friend Eleazer Wheelock. Wheelock would go on to found a charity school for Native Americans and also Dartmouth College. For now, he was a revivalist and associate of Edwards. Wheelock had just visited with Edwards at Northampton a few weeks prior, and perhaps he urged Edwards to ascend the pulpit. Tradition has it that Edwards was not expected to preach on this day at Enfield and that he stood in as a substitute. He had a sermon manuscript on a text from Deuteronomy 32:35 that he had recently preached at Northampton. He quickly made some revisions and on July 8, 1741, delivered perhaps the most famous sermon in American history: "Sinners in the Hands of an Angry God."

Stephen Williams, Edwards's cousin and fellow minister at Longmeadow, Massachusetts, also happened to be in attendance that day in Enfield. He recorded the extraordinary event in his diary:

> We went over to Enf[ield] where we met dear Mr. E[dwards] of N[orthhampton] who preachd a most awakening sermon from these words—Deut. 32:35 and before sermon was done—there was great moaning and crying out through ye whole House—"What Shall I do to be savd," "Oh I am going to hell," "Oh what shall I do for Christ," etc. So that ye

minister was obliged to desist—ye shrieks and crys were piercing & Amazing—After sometime of waiting the Congregation were still so that a prayer was made by Mr. W[heelock] and after that we descended from the pulpit and discoursed with the people—Some in one place and some in another and Amazing and Astonishing the power of God was seen—& Several Souls were hopefully wrought upon that night, & oh ye cheerfulness and pleasantness of their circumstances that receivd comfort—oh that God would strengthen and confirm—we sung an hymn & prayd & dismissd ye Assembly.

We might remember that in *Religious Affections* Edwards considers such outward manifestations to be no certain sign of a genuine converting work of God. One other account of the event notes that Edwards was careful not to resort to theatrics in his presentation in order to keep the congregation from getting too excited. He kept his voice at a monotone, and when he looked up from his sermon manuscript, he kept his eyes on the bell-rope. Additionally, he paused throughout the sermon and waited for his auditors to regain composure.

If the power was not in the presentation, then it certainly was in the words of this sermon. As Edwards carefully and vividly portrayed the wrath of God and the plight of sinners, those who heard his words realized full well their true condition. Revival had come to Enfield.

## Dangling Spiders and Open Doors

This sermon not only impacted the congregation that day, but it continues to leave its mark, and on a much wider audience. Perhaps no other sermon in the history of America has made more of an impact than Edwards's "Sinners in the Hands of an Angry God." One has to look fairly hard to find an anthology of American literature that does not include this sermon. Typically, however, it gets marked as an easy target for those wishing to depict the Puritans as hell-bent prophets of gloom and doom.

Edwards uses the image of a spider—putting his earlier observations of the flying spider to use again—dangling over a flame to represent our precarious position. Edwards likens one's slide toward eternal punishment to a heavy lead weight that sinks and plunges toward a bottomless gulf. Great waters being dammed up are employed to illustrate the impending rush of God's judgment. Finally, Edwards finds that God has bent the bow of his wrath and pointed the arrow of his justice at the unrighteous. To be sure, Edwards paints a picture of despair, and he refuses to whitewash either the condition or the reward awaiting the unrighteous. And these are the images in "Sinners" that most people remember.

Yet, to leave Edwards's sermon as simply dangling the spider over the pit would be like leaving a painting unfinished or a book half read. There is more to the story. He also employs another image that often gets overlooked. He declares to those slipping and sliding along their way: "Now you have an extraordinary opportunity, a day wherein Christ has thrown the door of mercy wide open and stands in calling, and crying with a loud voice to poor sinners."

If we place ourselves along the Connecticut River Valley in the 1740s, we would realize that we are on the frontier. We would realize our danger and we would look to the sure place of protection, the fortress. If we try, we can probably picture the large doors leading into the safety and security provided by the fort. Perhaps this is the image that Edwards wanted his readers to take away from this sermon, that is, the image of a grand door of mercy, turning on its great hinges. And through this door, Edwards declares that one can "see so many others feasting, while you are pining and perishing." But, Edwards was aware that our true need is

best seen in light of our true condition. And before he issues the call to come through the door of mercy, he paints
the picture of sin in all its harsh reality.

## The Art of Preaching

One scholar has remarked that the sermon is the primary
literary genre for Edwards. Very few of his ideas did not first
find public expression in one of his sermons. This, of course,
is not surprising, as Edwards's primary vocation was pastor.
Edwards had learned to preach from his father and from
Solomon Stoddard. He also learned from textbooks on
preaching that were a staple for Puritans. The chief textbook
was William Perkins's *The Art of Prophesying* (1592). This text
presented the hallmark structure of Puritan sermons, namely,
text, doctrine, and application. This structure, identified as
the "plain style," is readily identifiable in Edwards's sermons,
including "Sinners in the Hands of an Angry God."

Edwards also learned from the Puritan style that a sermon
should engage the whole person, both mind and heart. Edwards did not resort to rhetorical ornamentation as a gim-
mick or as a trick to manipulate the emotions. But, he did not
view the sermon as a purely intellectual exercise for preacher
and auditor alike. Sermons should be intellectually rigorous
and challenging, as Edwards often developed many points illustrating the rational character of spiritual truth. And, they
should also move the hearer from his or her complacency;
they should bring a response from the whole person.

This was Edwards's ambition in preaching. On the one
hand, he sought to avoid emotionalism and the haranguing
that came to identify so many revivalists of his time and continues to mark preachers to this day. On the other hand, he
aspired to avoid a detached and cold recital. Edwards accomplished this through allowing the truth to speak force-

fully. And "Sinners" stands as perhaps his finest attempt to utilize this strategy.

The sermon, as mentioned above, follows the pattern of text, doctrine, and application. Edwards chose Deuteronomy 32:35 as his text. Actually, he centered in on one phrase from this text, "In due time their foot will slip." He proceeds to set this phrase in its context and draw four observations regarding the impending doom that this phrase illustrates. The subjects of the text, the unrighteous Israelites, "were always exposed to sudden unexpected destruction." The only reason they are not fallen already is that "God's appointed time is not come." This naturally leads to the doctrine, which, also in Puritan fashion, Edwards presents in a single, declarative sentence: "There is nothing that keeps wicked men at any one moment out of hell, but the mere pleasure of God."

## No Security for a Moment

After Edwards states the doctrine, he devotes the next section of the sermon to considering its implications. He draws no fewer than ten specific points to flesh out the contours of this terrible, yet fundamental truth. His first point is that God does not lack the power to cast the wicked into hell. Unlike human sovereigns, who sometimes meet with resistance when attempting to overcome rebels and enemies, God is not hampered by a lack of power. This thought humbles Edwards, and he reminds his listeners of the necessary perspective on God's ability to judge. He notes, "What are we, that we should think to stand before him, at whose rebuke the earth trembles, and before whom the rocks are thrown down?"

Edwards then explains that God's justice demands that he punish the wicked, and the delay in carrying out his judgment is due solely to God's mercy. In fact, in the next several points, Edwards makes the observation that the wicked already stand condemned and are already objects of God's wrath. Only God in his mercy restrains sin from entirely consuming humanity. Edwards expresses the horrors of sin in the following:

> Sin is the ruin and misery of the soul; it is destructive in its nature; and if God should leave it without restraint, there would need nothing else to make the soul perfectly miserable. The corruption of the heart of man is immoderate and boundless in its fury; and while wicked men live here, it is like fire pent up by God's restraints, whereas if it were let loose, it would set on fire the course of nature; and as the heart is now a sink of sin, so, if sin was not restrained, it would immediately turn the soul into a fiery oven, or a furnace of fire and brimstone.

Edwards takes sin quite seriously. He does not gloss over its true nature and its effects. Some might read these words and take Edwards to be a consummate pessimist and naysayer. In reality, Edwards is a realist. Before he can express God's mercy through Christ, he is compelled to show our true need. One reason Edwards takes so much time in graphically portraying our true condition concerns our remarkable ability to evade, to ignore our true condition. We have grown rather skillful at covering up, and we have mastered the art of self-deception. We have anesthetized ourselves to our true condition and end. Edwards refers to this in his last few points, developing the doctrine as "false security." Edwards reminds us, however, that there "is no security to wicked men for one moment."

Sometimes this false security comes through accomplishments, work, or play. Sometimes, it comes through advances in medicine and science, in that they offer salvation

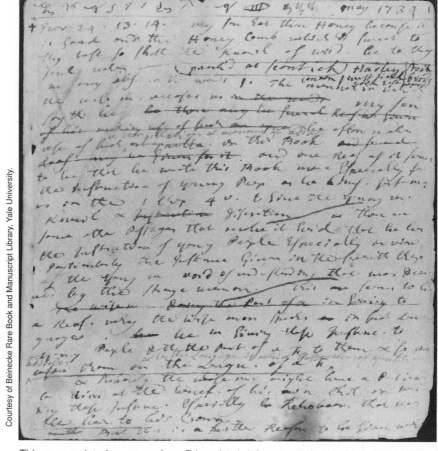

Courtesy of Beinecke Rare Book and Manuscript Library, Yale University.

This manuscript of a sermon from Edwards's brief pastorate in New York City during 1723 reflects his repeated editing. Pages of his sermon manuscript typically measure 4" x 4". On any given page Edwards managed to squeeze approximately twenty-eight lines of text, containing ten to twelve words each. He would sew the pages together to make a booklet.

from inevitable death. Edwards describes the futility of such efforts: "Natural man's prudence and care to preserve their own lives, or the care of others to preserve them, do not secure them for a moment."

Others think that somehow they will avoid the impending judgment. Again Edwards observes:

All wicked men's pains and contrivance which they use to escape hell, while they continue to reject Christ, and so remain wicked men, do not secure them from hell one moment. Almost every natural man that hears of hell, flatters himself that he should escape it; he depends upon himself for his own security; he flatters himself in what he has done, what he is now doing, or what he intends to do.

Edwards replies, however, that "the foolish children of men miserably delude themselves in their own schemes, and in confidence in their own strength and wisdom; they trust to nothing but a shadow." Edwards concludes: "Thus it is that natural men are held in the hand of God over the pit of hell; they have deserved the fiery pit, and are already sentenced to it." In other words, Edwards takes us back to his starting point in this section of the sermon, having demonstrated that "there is nothing that keeps wicked men out of hell, but the mere pleasure of God."

## The Wrath of Almighty God

When Edwards reaches the application section of this sermon, he gets quite personal. He turns as it were from the more polite second-person plural to the direct and unmitigated second-person singular. He does not allow one to think of somebody else who probably could use a good sermon like this one. Instead, he points the finger directly: "The use of this awful subject may be for awakening unconverted persons in this congregation."

Here Edwards unleashes his full arsenal of intense imagery to drive home the urgency of God's wrath. He exclaims:

There are the black clouds of God's wrath now hanging directly over your heads, full of the dreadful storm, and big with thunder; and were it not for the restraining hand of

God, it would immediately burst forth upon you. The sovereign pleasure of God, for a moment, stays his rough wind; otherwise it would come with fury, and your destruction would come like a whirlwind, and you would be like the chaff of the summer threshing-floor.

And then Edwards employs the illustration of the spider dangling over the pit: "The God that holds you over the pit of hell, much as one holds a spider, or some other loathsome insect, over the fire, abhors you, and is dreadfully provoked; his wrath towards you burns like fire." God's wrath is not one of his attributes that we ordinarily contemplate. In fact, we tend to gloss over it. Edwards, however, realizes that grasping the picture of God's wrath is the key to understanding fully the riches of his grace and the wonders of his love.

Edwards draws our attention to four characteristics of God's wrath. First, it is infinite because it is God's wrath. This again serves to humble us and causes us to stand in awe and fear of God.

Second, his wrath is fierce. Scripture describes God's wrath as exercised in fury, and exceedingly terrible. Here, however, Edwards points out, "Now God stands ready to pity you." God will pour out his wrath on his enemies, but now he is full of mercy and ready to pity poor sinners.

Third, God's wrath is proportionate to his love. As exceeding and abundant as his love is, so too is God's wrath. We much prefer to think of God's love, but we must see God in the fullness of his self-revelation. It's not about picking and choosing and having a made-to-order deity. God stands in the full revelation of his character and as real, and as central to his being as his love is, so is God's wrath.

And fourth, God's wrath, like his love, is eternal. An eternal separation from God and eternal suffering under his wrath are at stake. Edwards concludes, "How dreadful is the state of those that are daily and hourly in danger of this great wrath and infinite misery!"

## Come to Christ

But, Edwards's sermon does not stop there; he is not the hell-bent prophet of gloom and doom. All of this serves much like a preamble to his final and main point. As Edward Taylor so poetically put the matter, God "frowns with a smiling face." Edwards paints the picture of God's wrath and inevitable judgment of the wicked in order to emphasize both the need and wonder of Christ's mercy. The remainder of Edwards's sermon is reproduced below. In this final section of the application, Edwards stresses the need to come through the wide open door of mercy and to come to Christ. He reminds the listeners at Enfield of the work God is doing in neighboring towns, and mentions Suffield by name. He invites them to share in God's time of blessing as well:

And now you have an extraordinary opportunity, a day wherein Christ has thrown the door of mercy wide open, and stands in calling, and crying with a loud voice to poor sinners; a day wherein many are flocking to him, and pressing into the kingdom of God. Many are daily coming from the east, west, north, and south; many that were very lately in the same miserable condition that you are in, are now in a happy state, with their hearts filled with love to him who has loved them, and washed them from their sins in his own blood, and rejoicing in hope of the glory of God. How awful it is to be left behind at such a day! To see so many others feasting while you are pining and perishing! To see so many rejoicing and singing for joy of heart, and howl for vexation of spirit! How can you rest one moment in such a condition? Are not your souls as precious as the souls of the people of Suffield, where they are flocking from day to day to Christ?

He then turns to the various groups in the church and calls upon all—both young and old—to come to Christ. Edwards's challenge to children may be viewed as rather cruel, bordering on deliberately scaring children into heaven. Yet, if Edwards truly believes that those who die outside of Christ do in fact incur his wrath, then far from being cruel, Edwards is actually being as kind as he could be. He takes no pleasure in thinking about the future judgment. Rather, he desires that all, including the children, become the "holy and happy children of the King of Kings." So, he continues:

Are there not many here who have lived long in the world, and are not to this day born again? And so are aliens from the commonwealth of Israel, and have done nothing ever since they have lived, but treasure up wrath against the day of wrath? Oh, Sirs, your case, in an especial manner, is extremely dangerous. Your guilt and hardness of heart is extremely great. Do not you see how generally persons of your years are passed over and left, in the present remarkable and wonderful dispensation of God's mercy? You had need to consider yourselves, and awake thoroughly out of sleep. You cannot bear the fierceness and wrath of the infinite God. And you, young men and young women, will you neglect this precious season which you now enjoy, when so many others of your age are renouncing all youthful vanities and flocking to Christ? You especially have now an extraordinary opportunity; but if you neglect it, it will soon be with you as with those persons who spent all the precious days of youth in sin, and are now come to such a dreadful pass in blindness and hardness. And you, children, who are unconverted, do not you know that you are going down to hell, to bear the dreadful wrath of that God who is now angry with you every day and every night? Will you [be] content to be the children of the devil, when so many other children in the land are converted, and become the holy and happy children of the King of Kings?

And let everyone that is yet out of Christ, and hanging over the pit of hell, whether they be old men and women, or middle aged, or young people, or little children, now hearken to the loud calls of God's word and providence.

Edwards then makes the final point that God is presently doing a marvelous work, although, as he points out, this presents a catch-22. On the one hand, it is a marvelous testimony to the mercy and grace of God. On the other, the reverse dynamic can also take effect, as resistance during these times of invitation further hardens one's heart. His point both for those at Enfield and for us as well is never to presume upon the grace of God, and never to take his open door of mercy for granted. And so he concludes, calling upon his listeners to flee from the wrath of God:

This acceptable year of the Lord, a day of such great favor to some, will doubtless be a day of as remarkable vengeance to others. Men's hearts harden, and their guilt increases apace, at such a day as this, if they neglect their souls; and never was there so great danger of such persons being given up to hardness of heart and blindness of mind. God seems now to be hastily gathering in his elect in all parts of the land; and probably the greater part of adult persons that ever shall be saved, will be brought in now in a little time, and that it will be as it was on the great out-pouring of the Spirit upon the Jews in the apostle's days, the election will obtain, and the rest will be blinded. If this should be the case with you, you will eternally curse this day, and will curse the day that ever you was born, to see such a season of the pouring out of God's Spirit, and will wish that you had died and gone to hell before you had seen it. Now undoubtedly it is, as it was in the days of John the Baptist, the axe is in an extraordinary manner laid at the root of the trees, that every tree which brings forth not good fruit, may be hewn down, and cast into the fire.

Therefore, let every one that is out of Christ, now awake and fly from the wrath to come. The wrath of Almighty God is now undoubtedly hanging over a great part of this congregation. Let every one fly out of Sodom: "Haste and escape for your lives, look not behind you, escape to the mountain, lest you be consumed."

Edwards returns to the starting point, emphasizing the impending wrath of God. He has come full circle and along the way has tried to depict a full-orbed view of God: he overflows in mercy and pity and stands ready to forgive, and he abounds in wrath and fury and stands ready to condemn. Edwards preaches hard words that not all audiences, and especially audiences of today's sensibilities, are ready to hear. Edwards's understanding of sin and its consequences, however, only fills in half of the picture. For Edwards, the horrors of sin serve to magnify the grace of God; the condition of the wicked only serves to point to the need for Christ's mercy.

## Note on the Sources

"Sinners in the Hands of an Angry God" is found in every anthology of Edwards's writings, as well as in many anthologies of American literature and historical documents. It may be found in the Hickman edition of *The Works of Jonathan Edwards* (1834/1974), 2:7–12. It is included in *The Sermons of Jonathan Edwards: A Reader* (1999), pages 49–65. The sermon is also available in updated language in the booklet *Sinners in the Hands of an Angry God: Made Easier to Read* by John Jeffery Fanella (1996).

# 11

# A High Privilege
## *"The Most High, a Prayer-Hearing God"*

*Praise awaits you, O God, in Zion; to you our vows will
be fulfilled.
O you who hear prayer, to you all men will come.
When we were overwhelmed by sins, you forgave our
transgressions.
Blessed are those you choose and bring near to live in
your courts!
We are filled with the good things of your house, of your
holy temple.*
—Psalm 65:1–4

*The Most High is eminently a God that hears prayer*
—Jonathan Edwards,
"The Most High,
a Prayer-Hearing God"

Near the end of 1735, the cruel Northeast winter
took its toll on the colonial town of Boston: it
brought a great epidemic in which many fell ill
and many died. The epidemic spread to Northampton's
congregation, not so much directly as indirectly, as Edwards

and his parishioners mourned the loss of relatives and friends. A fast day was appointed and Edwards preached on prayer. Many had been praying already. Yet, as is often the case, after the season of prayer appeared to bring about no results, some began to question and to wonder.

Edwards looked upon this as an opportunity not only to address the subject of prayer, but also to explore God's character, God's will, and God's work in this world. Edwards offers some good answers to the questions that his congregation was asking under their breath by pointing them to the One who does in fact hear our prayers. In other words, Edwards anchors his thoughts on prayer in good theology.

One aspect of the contemporary church that would probably confound Edwards is the sharp distinction we make between theology and practical Christian living. Just as he argued for a holistic view of the self in *Religious Affections* and repudiated the distinction between the head and the heart, so he would argue for the necessary connection of theology to the Christian life. As this sermon illustrates so well, Edwards believed that the Christian life should be informed and shaped by a rigorous theology and also that theology should be enlivened by practice. They are mutually necessary, not mutually exclusive. So it is with this subject of prayer. In fact, Edwards's treatment of this subject is remarkable due entirely to the way he skillfully blends theology and practical Christian living together in this sermon.

Consequently, this is a fitting sermon to include in our tour of Edwards's life and thought. Here we see Edwards as a caring shepherd, acutely applying his knowledge of God and his Word to those in need, and he does so in a timely and convincing manner. He addresses many dimensions of prayer in this sermon. Chief among them is the way prayer reveals the uniqueness of God. Idols don't see, hear, and answer prayer. They have no idea of the needs or desires of the petitioner, and they have no power or ability to meet those needs. Conversely, God knows our needs before we even voice them.

Edwards also asks the obvious question, Why pray? This question raises a very practical point, and it is especially applicable due to Edwards's high view of the sovereignty of God. If God has foreordained whatsoever comes to pass and, as we noted in the discussion of *Freedom of the Will*, he will bring it to pass, then why pray? What good will it do? The short answer is that prayer perhaps has more to do with us than it does with God. For the long answer, we need to take a closer look at Edwards's sermon.

## The God Who Hears

After Edwards reads the text for this sermon, Psalm 65:2, "O you who hear prayer, to you all men will come," he offers a brief exposition. He notes that this is a psalm of thanksgiving and praise to God. Edwards further infers that it probably follows on the heels of David's petitioning of God concerning some deeply troubling circumstance that caused David to plead his case before God. Evidently, God answered David's prayer and so David offers his praise.

From this text, Edwards notes, "Hence we gather this doctrine, *that it is the character of the Most High, that he is a God who hears prayer.*" He then develops this doctrine by examining what is meant by the fact that God hears prayer. First, he points out that God accepts our prayers "as an offering to him." And they are offerings that please him. In fact, God "acts agreeably to his acceptance." In other words, he delights and takes pleasure in accepting our petitions. And sometimes, Edwards argues, in those times of prayer God enables us "to rest in him," in his grace, sovereignty, and sufficiency. Edwards turns to an example of this in 1 Samuel 1:

> [Hannah] came and poured out her soul before God, and spake out of the abundance of her complaint and grief; then we read, that she went away and did eat, and her countenance was no more sad, ver. 13, which seems to have been from some refreshing discoveries which God made of himself to her, to enable her to quietly submit to his will, and trust in his mercy, whereby God manifested his acceptance of her.

Edwards continues to unfold how God delights in answering prayer by stressing the free access that he has granted to his throne of mercy. "He sits on a throne of grace," Edwards observes, "and there is no veil to hide his throne, and keep us from it." Not only does God allow us to come to him, "but he encourages and frequently invites [us]; yea, manifests himself as delighting in being sought by prayer." Edwards further notes that God also answers prayers liberally. He contrasts this with human tendencies toward stinginess:

> Men often show their backwardness to give, both by the scantiness of their gifts, and by upbraiding those who ask of them. They will be sure to put them in mind of some faults, when they give them anything; but, on the contrary, God both gives liberally, and upbraids us not with our undeservings. He is plenteous and rich in his communications to those who call on him.

Because God hears and answers prayers, Edwards argues that "herein the most high God is *distinguished* from the false gods." Idols, or as Edwards refers to them "mere stocks and stones," are made with ears, but they don't hear, and they are made with eyes, but they don't see. Conversely, the true

God sees and hears. In fact, Edwards notes that he "perfectly knows the circumstances of everyone that prays to him throughout the world." He continues with the thought, causing us to ponder how marvelous God's hearing of our prayers really is, as he observes, "Though millions pray to him at once, in different parts of the world, it is no more difficult for him who is infinite in knowledge, to take notice of all than of one alone." God's perfect knowledge also means that "he doth not need to be informed by us, in order to [have] a knowledge of our wants, for he knows what things we need before we ask him."

Idols are "but vanities and lies; in them is no help." God, however, stands both ready and abundantly able to meet our needs; in him is help. But, this raises the question of why we should pray in order to enjoy God's blessings. Edwards asks the question this way, "Why doth God require prayer in order to the bestowment of mercies?"

## Why Pray?

Edwards first points out that we do not pray in order to inform God of our needs: "He is omniscient, and with respect to his knowledge, unchangeable. God never gains any knowledge by information." In reality, he knows our own needs better than we do ourselves, even before we voice them.

Also, we do not pray in order to change God's mind. Edwards admits, "God is sometimes represented as if he were moved and persuaded by the prayers of his people; yet it is not to be thought that God is properly moved or made willing by our prayers." Edwards reasons that just as it is impossible, due to God's omniscience, for God to gain any knowledge, so "it is no more possible that there should be any new inclination or will in God."

Nevertheless, Edwards observes, "God has been pleased to constitute prayer to be antecedent to the bestowment of mercy, and he is pleased to bestow mercy in consequence of prayer, as though he were prevailed upon by prayer." In other words, God ordains the end or the results, and he also ordains the means. Prayer is a God-ordained means to carrying out his will. Although this humbles us, God ordains the means of the prayers of his people in the carrying out of his will. We don't pray to change his mind; we pray so that we can be used of him.

Edwards further answers the question, Why pray? by drawing attention to how prayer changes us. God wants us to ask of him through prayer so that we acknowledge and fully realize our absolute dependence on him. Edwards expresses it this way:

> That we, when we desire to receive any mercy from him, should humbly supplicate the Divine Being for the bestowment of that mercy, is but a suitable acknowledgment of our dependence upon the power and mercy of God for that which we need, and but a suitable honour paid to the Author and Fountain of all good.

Prayer also changes us by preparing us for the work that God will do and the blessing he will give. "The mind," Edwards says, "is more prepared to prize [God's mercy], to rejoice in it when bestowed, and to be thankful for it." Prayer helps us to be mindful of our dependence upon God in both the asking and the receiving. So our prayers "excite in us a suitable sense and consideration of our dependence on God for the mercy we ask, and a suitable exercise of faith in God's sufficiency, that so we may be prepared to glorify his name when the mercy is received."

Finally, prayer teaches us about God's character and ours. God's hearing and answering our prayers speaks volumes about his nature. It announces his grace and heralds his goodness. It also points to his mercy in light of our unworthiness; it highlights his all-sufficiency in light of our weakness. Prayer reminds us that the Most High "is a God of infinite grace and mercy." And it reminds us of our desperate need for it. Edwards also reminds us, however, that in prayer we do not learn about God the Father alone.

## Christ's Purchase

Edwards's next move in the sermon reveals one of the overarching themes in his writings and thought: the supremacy and excellency of Christ. Edwards gets at this wonderful truth by examining Christ's role as high priest. In this role, Christ serves as our mediator through his work of atonement and intercession. Edwards brings these two works of Christ together in order to show how prayer is possible through Christ's mediatorial role. Edwards first draws attention to Christ's work of atonement, observing that "[Christ] hath by his blood made atonement for sin; so that our guilt need not stand in the way, as a separating wall between us and God, and that our sins be not a cloud through which our prayers cannot pass." Through Christ's atonement the dividing wall has been torn down and the clouds have been lifted.

If it had not been for Christ's work of atonement, Edwards argues that "our guilt would have remained as a wall of brass to hinder our approach." But, "Christ by his obedience, purchased this privilege, viz., that the prayers of those who believe in him should be heard." Christ's costly work on the cross purchased redemption from sin, and it also purchased the privilege of prayer.

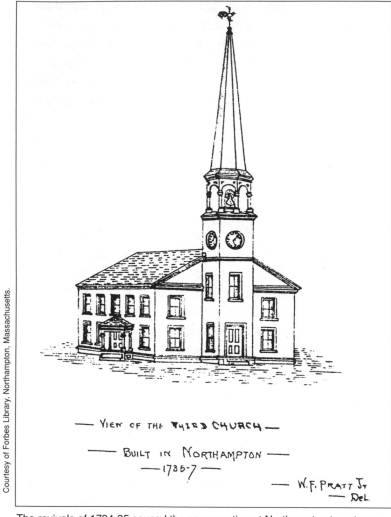

— VIEW OF THE THIRD CHURCH —

— BUILT IN NORTHAMPTON —
—1735-7—

— W. F. PRATT Jr
— DEL.

The revivals of 1734-35 caused the congregation at Northampton to outgrow its church. A new church was built from 1735 to 1737. Drawing attributed to William Pratt, 1874.

Christ's work of intercession also factors into the equation of prayer. In fact, Edwards notes that "Christ enforces the prayers of his people, by his intercession at the right hand of God in heaven. . . . He makes continual intercession for all that come to God in his name; so that their prayers come to God the Father through his hands." Christ's work of both atonement and intercession was purchased on the cross and brought with it the wonderful privilege of prayer.

The author of Hebrews points to this work of Christ as our ongoing mediator throughout the epistle. In Hebrews the author actually brings together both Christ's finished work of atonement and his ongoing work of intercession:

> Therefore, since we have a great high priest who has gone through the heavens, Jesus the Son of God, let us hold firmly to the faith we possess. For we do not have a high priest who is unable to sympathize with our weaknesses, but we have one who has been tempted in every way, just as we are—yet was without sin. Let us then approach the throne of grace with confidence, so that we may receive mercy and find grace to help us in our time of need. (Heb. 4:14–16)

The author of Hebrews also adds that Christ "always lives to intercede for [us]" (Heb. 7:25). As Edwards concludes, "We have a glorious Mediator, who has prepared the way, that our prayers may be heard consistently with the honour of God's justice and majesty."

## Our Privilege

When Edwards makes it to the application section of the sermon, his first thought is to stress how highly privileged we are to be able to pray to a prayer-hearing God. "The greater part of mankind are destitute of this privilege," he reminds us. "Whatever their necessities are, whatever their calamities or sorrows, they have no prayer-hearing God to whom they may go." But we "have the true God made known to us; a God of infinite grace and mercy; a God full of compassion to the miserable, who is ready to pity us under all troubles and sorrows, to hear our cries, and to give us all the relief which we need." No matter what the difficulty or concern, we can take it to God and find comfort, encouragement, mercy, and grace.

So, why do we neglect prayer, and why are we so careless with our high privilege? Edwards responds by pointing out that sometimes we are negligent in praying because our prayers don't always get answered. He does not offer this as an excuse. Nevertheless, he is well aware of the reality of unanswered prayer, and he takes the time in his application to deal with this issue.

Edwards outlines three responses to the problem of unanswered prayer. First, he notes the obvious reason. But, we are typically not so quick to admit it of ourselves. The reason that God does not answer some prayers is that we are desiring things "for no good end." Usually this is the case in relation to what Edwards refers to as "temporal things." It can, however, be applied more broadly. God does not answer such prayers because to do so, "he would act as his own enemy." For that matter, he would be acting as our enemy as well. Edwards cites James 4:3, which expresses the idea this way: "When you ask, you do not receive, because you ask with wrong motives, that you may spend what you get on your pleasures."

For God to answer such prayers would be self-defeating and contrary to his will for our lives. It's not always easy, however, to acknowledge this about our prayers. Edwards's words, however, remind us of the need to think about what we are asking, to inspect our motives, and to examine our hearts.

A second reason that God does not answer prayer relates to our insincerity or lack of faith. Edwards refers to this type of prayer as "an unbelieving prayer." We pray, but we don't really expect God to work. Typically, especially in the age of the televangelist, this gets applied to building grandiose buildings or reaping financial windfalls from heaven. Nothing could be further from Edwards's intentions as he relates this insincerity especially to overcoming areas of sin in our lives. Edwards explains it this way:

> Sometimes they pray for that in words which they really desire not in their hearts; as that he would purge them from sin, when at the time they show by their practice, that they do not desire to be purged from sin, while they love and choose it, while they are utterly averse to parting with it.

Edwards calls up short such insincere prayers. He reminds us that the all-seeing God can see "between real prayers and pretended ones." Edwards also applies his notion of insincere prayers to the dynamic of praying for something when we are truly relying on our own power and sufficiency to accomplish it. He notes that those who offer such prayers pretend to show dependence on God and reliance on his all-sufficiency, when in reality, "all the while, they trust in themselves, and have no confidence in God." Edwards offers a poignant illustration that shows how God sees right through this as well: "They show in words as though they were beggars; but in heart they come as creditors, and look on God as their debtor."

Edwards concludes his thought on this point by expressing the importance of praying by faith: "Prayer is a show or manifestation of dependence on God, and trust in his sufficiency and mercy. Therefore, where this trust or faith is wanting, there is no prayer in the sight of God."

Edwards's third and final response to the problem of unanswered prayer may be summed up in the idea of timing. As Edwards explains, "It is no argument that he is not a prayer-hearing God, that he exercises his own wisdom as to the time and manner of answering prayer." Sometimes when we pray, we fail to leave the timing in God's hands, we fail to realize that "the business of prayer is not to direct God." Because he is infinitely wise, God "knows what is best for us ten thousand times better than we, and knows what time and what way are best."

Not only does the timing rest with God, but also the details and contours of the answer rest with him as well. "God can answer prayer," Edwards reminds us, "though he bestow not the very thing we ask for." He continues:

> If our end [of our prayer] be our own good and happiness, God can perhaps better answer that end in bestowing something else than in the bestowment of that very thing which we ask. And if the main good we aim at on our prayer be attained, our prayer is answered, though not in the bestowment of the individual thing which we sought.

In other words, God always answers prayer, just not always according to our timing, and not always exactly as we think he should. God does not fail to hear and to answer prayer, even though we sometimes think differently.

In the end, apparently unanswered prayer is no excuse not to pray. Edwards ends his application section by reminding us again that prayer is a privilege. As a privilege, it stands in direct proportion to the price that purchased it. The privilege of prayer comes with the price of nothing less than the blood of Christ on the cross.

Privileges also involve responsibility. Since we are given the privilege of prayer, Edwards reasons that we have the duty to pray. So he concludes:

> If we enjoy so great a privilege as to have the prayer-hearing God revealed to us, how great will be our folly and inexcusableness, if we neglect the privilege, or make no use of it, and deprive ourselves of the advantage of not seeking this

God by prayer. They are hereby reproved who neglect the great duty of secret prayer, which is more expressly required in the word of God than any other kind.

Edwards refers to secret prayer, which is his way of saying private prayer. This activity of private prayer was viewed by Edwards as a crucial component of living the Christian life. Shortly after he arrived at Stockbridge, Edwards wrote a letter to a distinguished politician and military leader in Massachusetts, Sir William Pepperell. In the letter, Edwards sketches his philosophy of religious education for the school for Mohawks and Mohicans in Stockbridge. He stresses public worship on the Sabbath, daily family worship, and catechism classes. He also adds, "particular care should be taken to teach and direct each child, concerning the duty of *secret prayer*, and the duty pressed and enforced on everyone, and care should be taken, that all may have proper opportunity and convenience for it."

Edwards considered this activity to be essential, so he poses a rather probing question: "What account can those persons give of themselves, who neglect so known a duty?" Edwards does not need to answer this question, for there is no account that one could possibly give. He then exhorts us that since we have such a prayer-hearing God, our response should be rather simple: we should pray. He offers this final admonition:

> Let us be much employed in the duty of prayer; let us pray with all prayer and supplication; let us live prayerful lives, continuing instant in prayer, watching thereunto with all perseverance; praying always without ceasing, earnestly, and not fainting.

Edwards was stunned by the beauty, harmony, and excellency of God. This idea fills his writings and overflows in his sermons. During the years 1735 and 1736, God used these sermons and this idea to bring revival to the Connecticut River Valley and to Edwards's Northampton congregation. In this sermon on prayer, Edwards also stresses the excellency of God. Edwards embeds prayer, a fundamental activity of the Christian life, in a deeply theological context. He reminds us that, despite appearances, God does hear and answer prayer. Further, by requiring and commanding prayer, God reminds us that we are absolutely dependent upon him and his grace and mercy. Finally, Edwards reminds us that God's hearing of our prayers comes at a high price, as it was purchased through the atonement of Christ.

God alone is a prayer-hearing God. The activity of prayer proves this. It points to his uniqueness, his infinite grace and mercy, and his all-sufficient power. Prayer, perhaps like no other activity, heralds the excellency of God.

### Note on the Sources

Not as popular or well-known as other sermons of Edwards, "The Most High, a Prayer-Hearing God" is not available in many editions of his writings. It may be found, however, in the Hickman edition of *The Works of Jonathan Edwards* (1834/1974), 2:113–118. The letter to Sir William Pepperell may be found in George S. Claghorn's *Letters and Personal Writings* (1998), volume 16 of the Yale edition of *The Works of Jonathan Edwards*, pages 406–14.

# 12

# A GLORIOUS CELEBRATION

## *"Heaven Is a World of Love"*

*Love never fails. But where there are prophecies, they will cease; where there are tongues, they will be stilled; where there is knowledge, it will pass away. For we know in part and we prophesy in part, but when perfection comes, the imperfect disappears.*

—1 Corinthians 13:8–10

*If heaven be such a blessed world, then let this be our chosen country, and the inheritance we seek.*

—Jonathan Edwards,
*Charity and Its Fruits*

In 1738 Edwards embarked on a series of fifteen sermons on Paul's poetic hymn to the highest Christian virtue. Love or, following the Authorized Version, charity, would come to represent for Edwards the "essence of all true religion," by the time he writes *Religious Affections*. Love, for Edwards, is the tell-tale sign of genuine religious affections. Here, in the sermon series he entitled *Charity and Its Fruits,*

Edwards is only beginning his exploration of this profound concept and its implications for Christian living and ethics.

The revivals of 1735 and 1736 had passed, and the revivals associated with the Great Awakening were far off on the horizon. The demands for Edwards to travel and preach above and beyond his duties at Northampton had subsided and it would be a few years before they would pick up again. During this time between the revivals Edwards developed two systematic and extensive sermon series: this series on 1 Corinthians 13 and his ambitious thirty-sermon series on Isaiah 51:8, *History of the Work of Redemption*. As with *History of the Work of Redemption*, Edwards also likely planned someday to prepare this series for publication. But those plans never materialized.

These sermons would remain simply as manuscripts until 1851, when Tryon Edwards, his grandson, prepared them for publication. In the preface, Tryon Edwards notes that these lectures, even though they were not published by Edwards, rank among such works as *Freedom of the Will*, *Religious Affections*, and *History of the Work of Redemption*. Tryon Edwards remarks that these lectures "are marked throughout by that strong and clear thought, those broad and comprehensive views of truth, that thorough knowledge of human nature, and that accurate and familiar acquaintance with the Scriptures, which characterize the works of their familiar author."

Tryon Edwards also notes that the subject of these sermons "is eminently practical and important." He outlines the many aspects and wonders of love that his grandfather displays throughout the sermon, referring to love as "the first outgoing of the renewed soul to God," "the sure evidence of a saving work of grace," "the fullness and completeness of Christian character," and as that by which the saints "become like their Father in heaven, and fitted for his presence." Edwards develops all of these ideas from Paul's masterful chapter on love, which he refers to as "the greatest of these" (1 Cor. 13:13).

## The Greatest of These

Edwards begins *Charity and Its Fruits* with the same emphasis found in *Religious Affections.* As love is the "essence of all true religion" in *Religious Affections,* here it is "the sum of all virtue." In fact, this becomes the doctrine of the first sermon, which more fully stated, reads: "All that virtue which is saving, and distinguishing of true Christians from others, is summed up in Christian or divine love." "Let a man have what he will," reasons Edwards, "and let him do what he will, it signifies nothing without charity."

In this foundational sermon, Edwards takes time to explain what he means by divine love and to show how the roots of love sink deeply into God's character. This type of love requires the Spirit of God. The unregenerate, or Paul's "natural man," simply lacks the ability and capacity for such love. But what is this love that the Spirit produces?

Edwards observes that this love is a "disposition or affection by which one is dear to another." Remember from *Religious Affections* that affections do not equal emotions. When Edwards speaks of love, he is not thinking of the emotion. Instead, he is thinking of something deeper. He is thinking of one's whole life being lived, as it were, toward or for another. Ultimately this love is directed toward God. It also, however, is directed toward "our fellow creatures."

Also central to Edwards's understanding of love is the concept of disinterest in the self. As Edwards explains, "When God is loved aright he is loved for his excellency, the beauty of his nature, especially the holiness of his nature." He also adds, "And it is from the same motive that the saints are loved; they are loved for holiness' sake." In other words, any personal motives are pushed aside and any selfish interests get overlooked. This love is for God, not because of something that he will do for us, and not because of something that we can gain by it. Rather, it is for God because of his holiness, and because it is the only fitting response. And this love for God, Edwards observes, "is the foundation of gracious love to men."

The seventh sermon in this series affords Edwards the opportunity to develop this idea more fully, as he notes that love is contrary to a selfish spirit. Before the fall, humanity had the capacity to look beyond itself, to find fulfillment and meaning in the Creator and through him in the creation. "But," Edwards observes, "as soon as [man] had transgressed, those nobler principles were immediately lost and all this excellent enlargedness of his soul was gone and he thenceforward shrunk into a little point." Humanity became "closely shut up within itself to the exclusion of others." Through redemption, we once again have the capacity to enlarge ourselves. We no longer have to be consumed by ourselves, and we no longer need to suffocate on ourselves. Christian love forces us to look beyond our self-interest to the interests and needs of others.

Edwards continues in the first sermon of the series to show how all other virtues and duties of the Christian life naturally flow from love. True love issues in obedience, trust, and respect. It causes one to rejoice in the other, and also to put away all pretense, show, and deception. Edwards, following Paul, also makes the point that exercising the other virtues without love amounts to hypocrisy and insincerity.

Edwards also argues for love as the sum of all virtue, as it circumscribes the law and the whole of the duties required in God's Word. Christ's own words in Matthew 22 exalt love to this position. Here love to God and neighbor both capture the heart and scan the breadth of the law. Paul's own words concur. Even among Paul's primary virtues of faith, hope, and love, it is love that abides and it is love that is the greatest of these.

And so Edwards lays the foundation for his sermons on this topic by establishing love as the sum of all virtue. He continues his journey through Paul's chapter exploring the contours of Christian or divine love until he comes to the ultimate expression of love, reached at the end of the journey of the Christian life, in heaven.

## When the Perfect Comes

Edwards chose 1 Corinthians 13:8–10 as his text for the final installment in the charity series. This passage begins with the words "Love never fails." He dealt with the implication of this verse in the previous sermon, emphasizing the eternal nature of Christian love. Here he turns his attention to the other part of this text involving Paul's distinction between the imperfect and the perfect. Edwards interprets Paul's use of these two words as representing stages of the church and individual Christians. Consequently, Edwards views the perfect as representing both the end of the individual Christian's life and glorification, as well as the end of the church militant, as the end of the world. In other words, "when the perfect comes" refers to heaven.

While Edwards acknowledges both aspects of the perfect, he argues that Paul focuses on the latter. This is the "glorious state of the church," enjoying its final destination and relishing in the ultimate fulfillment of God's plan. And in heaven, love never fails. In fact, as the succinct and compact "doctrine" for this sermon heralds, "Heaven is a world of love." Following the pattern of his other sermons, Edwards develops this doctrine by considering a number of things in relation to heaven in order to help us to better see that it is in fact a world of love.

C. S. Lewis once remarked that it's odd how we don't capitalize heaven, and he wondered if it is because we don't always think of it as a real place. Thinking about heaven does present difficulties. Sometimes it gets the imagination going in rather fanciful directions of ethereal abstractions. Other times, our materialistic tendencies take over and we construct a world not too unlike our own. In this sermon, Edwards asks this proverbial question, What will heaven be like? but he does not answer the question in the customary way. Edwards's description is more along the lines of what we will do and what we will be, as opposed to what we will have and what heaven will look like.

He begins by thinking about heaven's occupants and he first turns his attention to God. God, in the fullness of his being as Father, Son, and Holy Spirit, is the "fountain of love." This love overflows and is reflected in heaven's other occupants, the angels and saints. As love is the sum of all virtue on earth, so it is in heaven. Consequently, Edwards contemplates the "excellent circumstances" that heaven provides for the exercise of love. He considers these grand themes using six separate points. Below we will examine a few of them as Edwards helps us understand what heaven will be like.

## The Fountain of Love

Edwards notes that, while God is omnipresent and fills heaven and earth, he is "more especially to be in some places rather than others," and heaven is the place that God especially dwells. Heaven is God's "palace, or presence-chamber." But, Edwards quickly reminds us that God dwells in heaven in the fullness of his Trinitarian being:

> There dwells God the Father, who is the Father of mercies, and so the Father of Love, who so loved the world that he gave his only begotten Son. . . . There dwells Jesus Christ . . . the Mediator, by whom all God's love is expressed to the saints, by whom the fruits of it have been purchased, and through whom they are communicated, and through whom love is imparted to the hearts of all the church. . . . There is the Holy Spirit, the Spirit of divine love, in whom the very essence of God, as it were, all flows out or is breathed forth in love, and by whose immediate influence all holy love is shed abroad in the hearts of all the church.

As each member of the Trinity uniquely contributes to the source and nature of divine love in heaven, together they "are united in infinitely dear and incomprehensible love." The result is a "fountain [that] overflows in streams and rivers of love and delight, enough for all to drink at, and to swim in, yea, so as to overflow the world as it were with a deluge of love." And this, argues Edwards, "renders heaven a world of love; for God is the fountain of love, as the sun is the fountain of light."

If love flows from God's being, then it follows that it reflects his character. Consequently, Edwards notes that God's love is infinite, all-sufficient, and eternal:

> Therefore seeing he is an infinite Being, it follows that he is an infinite fountain of love. Seeing he is an all-sufficient Being, it follows that he is a full and overflowing and inexhaustible fountain of love. Seeing he is an unchangeable and eternal Being, he is an unchangeable and eternal source of love. There even in heaven dwells that God from whom every stream of holy love, yea every drop that is or ever was proceeds.

This love expressed within the Trinity then overflows to other occupants of heaven, the angels and the saints. Edwards exclaims: "All the persons who belong to that blessed society are lovely. The Father of the family is so, and so are all his children. The Head of the body is so, and so are all the members." The love that binds the Father to the Son and to the Holy Spirit binds God to his children. In fact, this mutual love results in the creation of the world and is the very reason for humanity's existence. The love expressed within the Trinity spills out, as it were, and desires the relationship of others. Edwards pictures heaven as the ultimate fulfillment of God's plan for the world and as an extraordinary union between God and his people.

**Excellent Circumstances**

Additionally, all members of this heavenly society are also pure and holy, "and shall be without blemish of sin or imprudence or any kind of failure." Consequently, the principle of love, which reigns in heaven, operates without any obstacles. Edwards develops this thought in his last two points of the sermon's doctrine section.

As Edwards notes, "Most of the love which there is in this world is of an unhallowed nature." Our insufficiencies and sin mar even our noblest attempts at loving God and loving others. At our worst, strife, contention, and enmity abound as we deal contemptuously with God, each other, and even ourselves. But in heaven, love proceeds "not from corrupt principles, not from selfish motives, and not to mean and vile purposes." Instead, there the saints "love God for his own sake, and each other for God's sake, for the sake of that relation which they bear to God, and that image of God which is upon them." The enclosed and suffocated self mentioned earlier is freed and enlarged to love God and others.

Edwards observes, "That which was in the heart as but a grain of mustard seed in this world shall there be as a great tree." Those times when we rise above ourselves and love God and others in this world are magnified exponentially in heaven; the times that we relish God and rejoice with others here will abound in heaven. "No envy," Edwards continues, "or malice, or revenge, or contempt, or selfishness shall enter there." Consequently, his final point in the doctrine section expresses "the excellent circumstances in which love shall be expressed and enjoyed in heaven."

He sketches this out by making ten subpoints. First, he notes that love is always mutual, and in heaven acts of love are returned. No one who exercises love "will ever be grieved that he is slighted by those whom he loves." There will be no unrequited love in heaven.

Second, the love exercised in heaven will "never be dampened or interrupted by jealousy." Additionally, flattery and pretense will also be absent. So, Edwards argues, "the saints shall know that God loves them, and they shall not doubt of the greatness of his love; and they shall have no doubt of the love of all their fellow heavenly inhabitants." It will be a love without suspicion and without question.

Third, while we have a great deal to hinder us here on earth, the saints will "have nothing within themselves to clog them in the exercises and expressions of love." A "lump of flesh and blood" now weighs us down. When the perfect comes, the hindrances of sin will be removed.

Fourth, even when we do love sincerely, we sometimes lack the wisdom or discretion as to the manner and circumstance of exercising love. We sometimes say and do the right things at the wrong time. And sometimes when our timing is right, the delivery goes awry. But in heaven, wisdom and discretion perfectly blend with love.

Fifth, and this point personally affected Edwards as he was separated from his children once they married, we will not have "the distance of habitation" hindering our love, for in heaven, the saints will "be together as one family in their heavenly Father's house."

Edwards's next five points concern the nature of heaven as the union of one family and one society. In heaven mutual respect, admiration, concern—in short, mutual love—reigns. We practice all of these things now, "but," as Edwards points out, "these are done much more perfectly in heaven."

In his last point, Edwards emphasizes the eternal nature of love in heaven:

> The paradise of love shall always be continued as in a perpetual spring. There shall be no autumn or winter; every plant there shall be in perpetual bloom with the same undecaying pleasantness and fragrancy, always springing forth, always blossoming, and always bearing fruit.

Heaven affords the perfect circumstances for the perfect exercise of altruistic, sincere, pure, and eternal love. While we enjoy God's love now and while we delight in the love of others, and while we reciprocate that love as best we can, such is only a foretaste of heaven and a glimpse of the love that will be expressed.

## On the Way to Heaven

Edwards's beatific vision, however, is not simply a message of hope for the future; it impacts the way we should live now. If our appetites are whetted for heaven and those excellent circumstances in the future, then we should live as if we were already there. Consequently, as this sermon turns to the application section, Edwards emphasizes the idea that we should earnestly seek after heaven. The message that "heaven is a world of love" also brings comfort as we "pass through difficulties" along the way.

He begins his application, however, with a challenge. Since love is the hallmark of Christianity, "this may lead us to see a reason why contention has such an influence as it has to darken persons' evidences for heaven." This works two ways. First, in the Christian who acts contentiously, it becomes a means of doubt and eclipses both assurance and the lively communion with God. Edwards observes, "So when converted persons get into ill frames in their families, the consequence commonly, if not universally, is that they live without much of a sense of heavenly things." He explains the logic of this dynamic: "For heaven being a world of love, it follows that when persons have the least exercise of love, and most of contrary principles, they have least of heaven and are farthest from it in their frames of mind."

Second, the other way that contention and the exercise of love's contrary principles darken the evidences of heaven relates to the unconverted. Contentious Christians and a contentious church obscure the glories of heaven. Like a heavy cloud, they darken the light of heaven's love. This, however, offers no excuse for those outside of Christ. Edwards solemnly addresses the unregenerate. He bluntly, but honestly, gives notice that none of the joy and love and wonder of heaven, "none of this belongs to you." The unregenerate stand at enmity with God and against all that heaven represents, and consequently will not "in any wise enter in there." While heaven is a world of love, "Hell is a world of hatred." As God's love without mixture reigns in heaven, so he pours out his unmingled wrath in hell.

As in "Sinners in the Hands of an Angry God," Edwards here paints a real picture of hell in order to awaken the unregenerate to their true condition. He adds: "These are no cleverly devised fables. They are the great and awful truths of God's word." And they are things that unfortunately will be made true. So he petitions, "Let the consideration of what has been said of heaven stir you up earnestly to seek after it."

He spends the majority of his time in the application section, however, addressing the implication for believers of the truth that heaven is a world of love. He reminds us that we should seek heaven and that our affections "must be taken off from the pleasures of the world." We must live like pilgrims, like citizens of another country. This mind-set, however, should not be looked upon as one of deprivation. The real treasures and joys are heavenly.

Edwards also realizes that the journey to heaven can be difficult. He extols the virtues of perseverance and reveals how this understanding of heaven serves to encourage us along the way:

> Be content to pass through all difficulties in the way to heaven. . . . That glorious city of light and love is, as it were, on the top of an high hill, an elevation which is exalted above the hill, and there is no arriving there without traveling uphill. Though this be wearisome, yet it is worth your while to come and dwell in such a glorious city at last. Be willing therefore to comply with this labor. What is it in comparison of the sweet rest which is at the end of your journey?

Finally, while only heaven affords the excellent circumstances for the perfect exercise of love, we should endeavor to live as close to the mark as we can while we are here on earth. "By living in love in this world the saints partake of like sort of inward peace and sweetness" to what inhabitants of heaven enjoy. "It is in this way," he continues, "that you are to have the foretastes of heavenly pleasures and delights." He then warns:

A contrary spirit, a spirit of hatred and ill will, greatly hinders a sense of those things. It darkens the mind and clouds such objects, and puts them out of sight. A frame of holy love to God and Christ, and a spirit of love and peace to men greatly disposes and fits the heart for a sense of the excellence and sweetness of heavenly objects. It gives a relish of them. It, as it were, opens the windows by which the light of heaven shines upon the soul.

He concludes that "as heaven is a world of love, so the way to heaven is the way to love." As mentioned in chapter 11, most people never get a glimpse of this Edwards, as they only see him dangling the spider over the pit of flames in "Sinners in the Hands of an Angry God." Here we gain a rather different picture of the colonial New England minister. This is not to suggest that Edwards did not take sin and its consequences seriously. He did, to be sure. It is to suggest, however, that Edwards's thought, and the gospel for that matter, contains both solemn warnings and good news. In the final sermon in his series *Charity and Its Fruits,* Edwards peels back heaven and reveals the harmony and delight of God and his people, helping us see heaven as a world of love.

It is fitting that we conclude our journey with the sermons of Edwards. These writings span his whole career and are the backbone to his thought. The three examples examined in part 4 only scratch the surface of the approximately 1,400 sermon manuscripts left behind by Edwards. Only a relatively short number have found their way into print. All of them attest to Edwards's desire to lead his congregations at New York, Northampton, and Stockbridge, as well as places where his many travels carried him, into a more penetrating knowledge of God, his Word, and his world.

Edwards skillfully weaves together his acute understanding of the biblical text and his theological and philosophical reflections with literary and rhetorical dexterity. He inherited a sermonic form and style from his Puritan forebears that he honed and developed. In the end, these sermons offer the listener and reader what Edwards hoped they would: a clearer picture of God in his excellency and a clearer picture of our fitting response in love and obedience.

## Note on the Sources

*Charity and Its Fruits* is not available in the Hickman edition of *The Works of Jonathan Edwards* (1834/1974) because *Charity* was not published until 1851. Tryon Edwards was the editor of this edition, which is available in a reprint edition (1969). The final sermon, "Heaven Is a World of Love," is found on pages 323–68. An edition based on a nineteenth-century manuscript copy from the Edwards collection at Andover-Newton Theological Seminary may be found in Paul Ramsey's *Ethical Writings* (1989), volume 8 of the Yale edition of *The Works of Jonathan Edwards*, pages 125–397; "Heaven is a World of Love" appears on pages 366–97. Finally, this sermon may also be found in *The Sermons of Jonathan Edwards: A Reader* (1999), pages 242–72.

# CONTINUING THE JOURNEY
## *A Brief Guide to Books by and about Jonathan Edwards*

As we mentioned in the introduction, this book is only the beginning. It serves to introduce the life and thought of Jonathan Edwards by exploring some of his well-known, and not so well-known, works. Some works have necessarily been left out. Among these are *The Two Dissertations: Concerning the End for which God Created the World & The Nature of True Virtue, The Great Christian Doctrine of Original Sin Defended,* and *Some Thoughts on the Present Revival of Religion.* Also left out are many of his well-known sermons, including "A Divine and Supernatural Light," numerous sermons on the excellency of Christ, and his final sermon at Northampton, which he simply entitled "A Farewell Sermon."

To cover all these works, plus his many others, would be a monumental, if not insurmountable, challenge. Reading his works, however, is a challenge worth taking up. Below follows a guide to the various available editions of Edwards's writings. I have also included a few noteworthy books about Edwards. The past fifty years have witnessed an explosion of books, articles, theses, and dissertations about his life and thought. Consequently, this list is only a sampling of the vast literature available on America's pastor, theologian, and philosopher, Jonathan Edwards.

## Books by Edwards

A comprehensive, although incomplete, edition of Edwards's works was reprinted by the Banner of Truth in 1974. *The Works of Jonathan Edwards,* a two-volume set edited by Edward Hickman, was first published in 1834. This edition also contains a thorough life of Edwards by Sereno E. Dwight, spanning over two hundred pages. Dwight's "Memoir" also reproduces portions from Edwards's letters and other writings.

Volume 1 includes many of Edwards's major treatises, including *Freedom of the Will, The Two Dissertations, Original Sin, Religious Affections,* the revival writings, and *History of the Work of Redemption.* Volume 2 contains primarily sermons, although it also includes *Distinguishing Marks of a Work of the Spirit of God,* Edwards's *Life of David Brainerd,* and some of Edwards's *Miscellanies* and shorter theological works.

The Banner of Truth makes many of Edwards's works available in smaller, paperback editions. These include a collection of sermons entitled *Jonathan Edwards on Knowing Christ* (1990); his revival writings entitled *Jonathan Edwards on Revival* (1984); the sermon series edited by Tryon Edwards, *Charity and Its Fruits* (1969); and *Religious Affections* (1986).

Under the leadership of the late Puritan historian and scholar Perry Miller, *The Works of Jonathan Edwards* committee and Yale University Press began producing a comprehensive, although still not complete, critical edition of his writings. The first volume appeared in 1957. All of these volumes contain rather lengthy introductions, discussions, and notes regarding manuscript issues. *The Works of Jonathan Edwards,* now under the leadership of Harry S. Stout and

Kenneth P. Minkema, intends to publish twenty-six volumes covering Edwards's major treatises, sermons, *Miscellanies* and notebooks, letters and personal writings, and the shorter writings. Eighteen volumes are available, with the remainder due to be published over the next few years.

Part of the renaissance of Edwards studies is due to the Yale edition of his works. When the set is complete, Edwards studies will more than likely continue to flourish. Yale University Press has made available two readers as a sample of this massive series: *A Jonathan Edwards Reader* (1995) and *The Sermons of Jonathan Edwards: A Reader* (1999).

Volumes in the Yale edition of *The Works of Jonathan Edwards* are rather expensive. While the serious scholar should consult all of them, some stand out for anyone interested in pursuing Edwards's thought: vol. 2, *Religious Affections*, edited by John E. Smith; vol. 4, *The Great Awakening*, edited by C. C. Goen; vol. 8, *Ethical Writings*, edited by Paul Ramsey; vol. 12, *Ecclesiastical Writings*, edited by David D. Hall; and vol. 16, *Letters and Personal Writings*, edited by George S. Claghorn.

## Books about Edwards

There are so many valuable works on Edwards that this list is necessarily quite selective. All of these books are helpful, and they point to the variety of scholarship one finds in this field.

First, biographies. Perry Miller's *Jonathan Edwards* (1949/1981) provides valuable analysis of Edwards's life, though not all agree with some of his conclusions. Iain H. Murray's *Jonathan Edwards: A New Biography* (1987) is a tour de force, patiently guiding the reader through the details of Edwards's life. George Marsden, known for his works on fundamentalism and evangelicalism, has been working for some time on a biography of Edwards. His work should appear in the near future and will be a welcome contribution.

One other work related to Edwards's life is the diary of his daughter Esther: *The Journal of Esther Edwards Burr,* edited by Carol Karlsen and Laurie Crumpacker (1984).

The magazine *Christian History* devoted an issue to Edwards (vol. 4, 1985), which contains helpful and interesting articles on his life, times, and thought.

*The Works of Jonathan Edwards* committee, in addition to producing Edwards's works, also sponsors conferences on Edwards and has produced a few anthologies of scholarly essays. One of these, *Jonathan Edwards and the American Experience,* edited by Nathan O. Hatch and Harry S. Stout (1988), offers essays on the thought of Edwards.

Other works worthy of mention concern Edwards's theology. Conrad Cherry offers an overview, noting Edwards's debt to John Calvin and correcting some of Miller's ideas, in *The Theology of Jonathan Edwards: A Reappraisal* (1990). John H. Gerstner produced a massive, three-volume work, *The Rational Biblical Theology of Jonathan Edwards* (1991–1993).

Other studies cover either specific works of Edwards or specific areas of his thought. Among these stand Gerald R. McDermott's *Seeing God: Twelve Reliable Signs of True Spirituality* (1995), a study of *Religious Affections.* Archie Parrish and R. C. Sproul's *The Spirit of Revival: Discovering the Wisdom of Jonathan Edwards* (2000) explores his revival writings. Finally, John Piper's book *God's Passion for His Glory: Living the Vision of Jonathan Edwards* (1998) focuses on *Concerning the End for which God Created the World.*

Of the many scholarly studies on the thought of Edwards, the following are noteworthy here: Norman Fiering's *Jonathan Edwards's Moral Thought and Its British Context* (1981); Gerald R. McDermott's *One Holy and Happy Soci-*

*ety: The Public Theology of Jonathan Edwards* (1992), an insightful analysis of Edwards's ethics and theology; and Michael J. McClymond's *Encounters with God: An Approach to the Theology of Jonathan Edwards* (1998), a rewarding treatment of Edwards's theology and apologetics.

The vast literature on Edwards testifies to his continuing relevance to the church. There is, in Murray's words, "an urgent need of a new generation to take up and read Edwards." Not simply, of course, to learn about him. He should not be read in order to be put on a pedestal. Edwards should be read and studied because he so clearly points beyond himself to our only sure guide in Scripture. He so forcefully and passionately reminds us to keep our eyes fixed on Christ, the Author and Finisher of our faith. Edwards challenges us through both the example of his life and the power of his writings to relish God, to enjoy and glorify him in this life and the life to come.

# BIBLIOGRAPHY

Burr, Esther Edwards. *The Journal of Esther Edwards Burr, 1754–1757.* Edited by Carol F. Karlsen and Laurie Crumpacker. New Haven: Yale University, 1984.

Cherry, Conrad. *The Theology of Jonathan Edwards: A Reappraisal.* Garden City, N.Y.: Anchor, 1966. Reprint ed. Bloomington: Indiana University, 1990.

Dwight, Sereno E. *Memoirs of Jonathan Edwards, A.M.* In *The Works of Jonathan Edwards.* Edited by Edward Hickman. 2 vols. 1834. 1:xi–cxcvii.

Edwards, Jonathan. *Charity and Its Fruits: Christian Love as Manifested in the Heart and Life.* Edited by Tryon Edwards. 1851. Reprint ed. Edinburgh/Carlisle, Pa.: Banner of Truth, 1969.

———. *Jonathan Edwards on Knowing Christ.* Edinburgh/Carlisle, Pa.: Banner of Truth, 1990.

———. *Jonathan Edwards on Revival.* Edinburgh/Carlisle, Pa.: Banner of Truth, 1984.

———. *A Jonathan Edwards Reader.* Edited by John E. Smith, Harry S. Stout, and Kenneth P. Minkema. New Haven: Yale University, 1995.

———. *Jonathan Edwards' Resolutions: And Advice to Young Converts.* Edited by Stephen J. Nichols. Phillipsburg, N.J.: P&R, 2001.

———. *Religious Affections.* Edinburgh/Carlisle, Pa.: Banner of Truth, 1986.

———. *The Sermons of Jonathan Edwards: A Reader.* Edited by Wilson H. Kimnach, Kenneth P. Minkema, and Douglas A. Sweeney. New Haven: Yale University, 1999.

———. *Sinners in the Hands of an Angry God.* Phillipsburg, N.J.: P&R, 1992.

———. *Sinners in the Hands of an Angry God.* Edited ("made easier to read") by John Jeffery Fanella. Phillipsburg, N.J.: P&R, 1996.

———. *The Works of Jonathan Edwards.* Edited by Edward Hickman. 2 vols. 1834. Reprint ed. Edinburgh/Carlisle: Banner of Truth, 1974.

――――. *The Works of Jonathan Edwards.* Edited by Perry Miller, John E. Smith, and Harry S. Stout. New Haven: Yale University, 1957– .
Vol. 1. *The Freedom of the Will.* Edited by Paul Ramsey. 1957.
Vol. 2. *Religious Affections.* Edited by John E. Smith. 1959.
Vol. 4. *The Great Awakening.* Edited by C. C. Goen. 1972.
Vol. 6. *Scientific and Philosophical Writings.* Edited by Wallace E. Anderson. 1980.
Vol. 8. *Ethical Writings.* Edited by Paul Ramsey. 1989.
Vol. 9. *A History of the Work of Redemption.* Edited by John F. Wilson. 1989.
Vol. 12. *Ecclesiastical Writings.* Edited by David D. Hall. 1994.
Vol. 16. *Letters and Personal Writings.* Edited by George S. Claghorn. 1998.

Fiering, Norman. *Jonathan Edwards's Moral Thought and Its British Context.* Chapel Hill: University of North Carolina/Williamsburg, Va.: Institute of Early American History and Culture, 1981.

Gerstner, John H. *The Rational Biblical Theology of Jonathan Edwards.* 3 vols. Powhatan, Va./Orlando: Ligonier Ministries, 1991–93.

Hatch, Nathan O., and Harry S. Stout, eds. *Jonathan Edwards and the American Experience.* New York/Oxford: Oxford University, 1988.

McClymond, Michael J. *Encounters with God: An Approach to the Theology of Jonathan Edwards.* New York/Oxford: Oxford University, 1998.

McDermott, Gerald R. *One Holy and Happy Society: The Public Theology of Jonathan Edwards.* University Park: Pennsylvania State University, 1992.

――――. *Seeing God: Twelve Reliable Signs of True Spirituality.* Downer's Grove, Ill.: InterVarsity, 1995.

Miller, Perry. *Jonathan Edwards.* New York: William Sloane, 1949. Reprint ed. Amherst: University of Massachusetts, 1981.

Murray, Iain H. *Jonathan Edwards: A New Biography.* Edinburgh/Carlisle, Pa.: Banner of Truth, 1987.

Parrish, Archie, and R. C. Sproul. *The Spirit of Revival: Discovering the Wisdom of Jonathan Edwards: With the Complete, Modernized Text of "The Distinguishing Marks of a Work of the Spirit of God."* Wheaton: Crossway, 2000.

Piper, John. *God's Passion for His Glory: Living the Vision of Jonathan Edwards: With the Complete Text of "The End for Which God Created the World."* Wheaton: Crossway, 1998.

# INDEX OF PERSONS

241

# INDEX OF EDWARDS'S WORKS

# INDEX OF SCRIPTURE